D0319748

THE FORTH RAILWAY BRIDGE

THE FORTH RAILWAY BRIDGE

A Celebration

by ANTHONY MURRAY
With CHARLES MACLEAN & SIMON SCOTT

MAINSTREAM
PUBLISHING

Copyright © Anthony Murray 1983
All rights reserved
First published 1983
This edition 1988
Reprinted 1989
Reprinted 1991

This edition published by
MAINSTREAM PUBLISHING COMPANY (EDINBURGH) LTD.
7 Albany Street,
Edinburgh EH1 3UG

ISBN 185158 123 5

No part of this book may be reproduced or transmitted in any form
or by any means, mechanical or electric, including photocopy,
recording, or any information storage or retrieval system now
known or to be invented, without permission in writing from the
publisher, except by a reviewer who wishes to quote brief passages
in connection with a review for insertion in a magazine, newspaper
or broadcast.

Cover design by James Hutcheson
Book design by Jenny Carter

Printed by Hollen Street Press Ltd
Bound by Hunter & Foulis Ltd, Edinburgh

British Library Cataloguing in Publication Data

Murray, Anthony,
    The Forth Railway Bridge.—2nd ed.
    1. Scotland. Firth of Forth. Railway
    bridges. Forth Bridge
    I. Title   II. Maclean, Charles, *1951-*
    III. Scott, Simon
    624'.37'094131

ISBN 1-85158-123-5

TO ALBURY

ACKNOWLEDGEMENTS

The author is very grateful for the kind help from the following:–

The Scottish Records Office
National Library of Scotland
Edinburgh Central Library
Royal Scottish Museum
Albury Sanders
Betty Finlay
Nicola Barry
George Cameron

Locomotive and General Railway Photographs.
F. Moore's Railway Photographs (Ian Allan)

ILLUSTRATIONS

Map on page 10 is from the Edinburgh Geographical Institute
Page 23 – Woodcut from the Illustrated London News
pp 28 & 29 – Early issues of The Railway Magazine
p 32 – The Edinburgh Central Library
pp 34 & 36 – Westhoven
p 39 – Royal Scottish Museum, Crown Copyright
p 41 – Royal Scottish Museum, Crown Copyright
p 44 – Royal Scottish Museum, Crown Copyright
p 47 – Westhoven
pp 48 & 49 – Westhoven
p 51 – Royal Scottish Museum, Crown Copyright
pp 52, 53 & 54 – National Library of Scotland
p 66 – The Railway Magazine
p 67 – Edinburgh Central Library
p 75 – Royal Scottish Museum, Crown Copyright
p 97 – The War Office

The Frontispiece and all the illustrations on the following pages are from the author's collection:
pp – 10, 33, 37, 38, 43, 55, 56, 70, 73, 74, 79, 80, 83, 84, 85, 86, 87, 88, 90, 92, 94, and 96.

CONTENTS

PIC-NIC ON THE BEACH—
ABERDOUR

An illustration from the 1912 edition of the North British Railway's Official Tourist Guide. The SILVER SANDS would be the correct title for this vista, since THE BEACH, proper, was round the corner to the left almost at right angles facing south. The Fife Coast railway line ran along the embankment at the back of the picture, and succeeding picture post-cards down the years showed progressive vegetation which now almost obscures the trains—a state of affairs which for the author's childhood picnics was fortunately far in the future.

There were no facilities for pleasure paddle steamers at the Silver Sands in real life.

INTRODUCTION

I was born in a staid South Edinburgh suburb before the first World War was over, and I have recollections of my early infancy with all its accompanying personal and intimate attention. Being too young to walk, I always seemed to be out and about in a pram and it was whilst suitably swaddled and supine that I caught my first glimpse of an airship.

At the foot of the long tree-lined road where we lived in those days, the Edinburgh Suburban and South Side Junction Railway ran under a wide bridge which carried a mingling of cable trams, horse traffic, pedestrians and primitive motor cars. The white smoke erupting from the low level railway trains fascinated me and I used to howl the place down when we were too late to see the train itself.

In addition to the railway near home, the real treat was our annual holiday, when the family took Emerald Cottage at the Fife seaside resort of Aberdour. I loved the noise and commotion at Waverley Station to be followed by crossing the Forth Bridge, which I thought had been put there for my benefit, and travelling through the North Queensferry tunnel which was usually threaded in complete darkness because the compartment gas lamps were not lit for early daytime travel. To me the whole journey of some 40 minutes seemed to take all day and was very much part of the holiday.

It was this annual pilgrimage to Aberdour which provided me with my first railway journeys. Everyone including some domestic help and Nanny would pile into a horse-

9

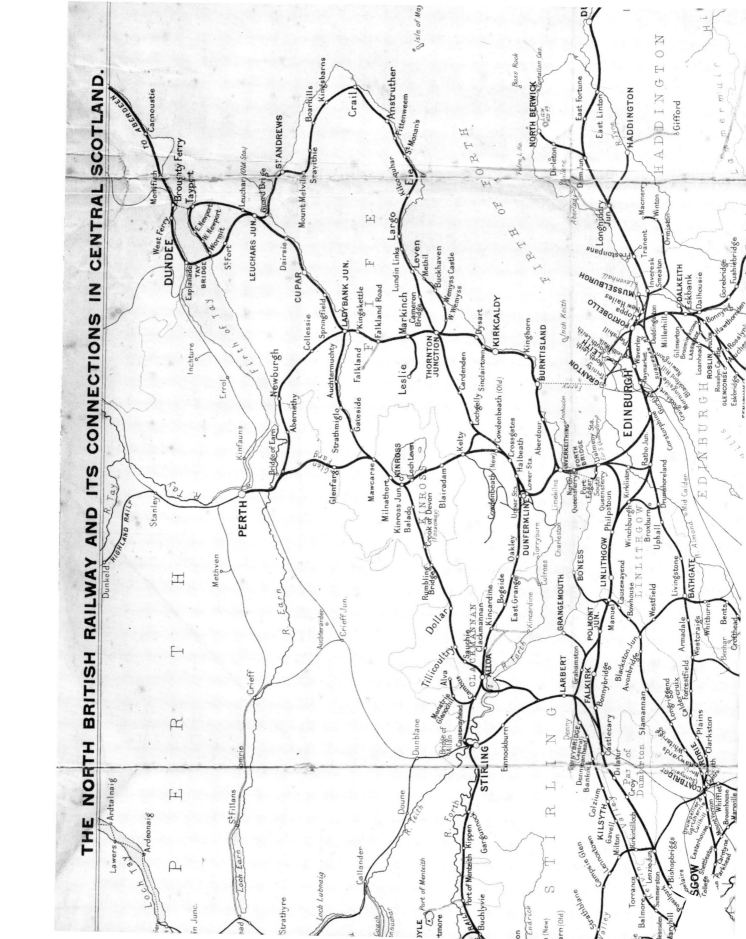

THE NORTH BRITISH RAILWAY AND ITS CONNECTIONS IN CENTRAL SCOTLAND.

drawn cab, and after much fuss and panic in case we missed the train we would finally alight at the station, where in those days there seemed to be ample porterage to cope with the family and all our luggage and paraphernalia.

Sometimes we entrained at Haymarket instead of Waverley. The platforms for the west and north bound trains at this through station are at the foot of staircases each riser of which as on early tram cars in those times was embellished with a red enamelled strip advertising Iron Jelloids. With four lines operating at full strength the din at Haymarket in steam days could be shattering. Most trains as now would stop there *en route*, but not all. An Aberdeen Express with a North British Railway Atlantic Locomotive at full throttle would burst forth from the tunnel and add to the inferno of noise, smoke and steam. Everyone was deafened and took fright; our Yorkshire terrier got hysterics, and I relished every minute of it. I used to be sorry to leave Haymarket, especially when I was old enough to be able to read the name plates on the various locomotives, but the Forth Bridge crossing was the real treat.

It would be interesting to know how a child today reacts, if at all, on being taken over the new Road Bridge. From a private car it is doubtful if he could be fully aware of his surroundings, being so near the ground on a wide roadway. He has no means of beholding his situation in awesome wonderment as we did of yore from the carriage window. From the near side it seemed as if we looked straight down over a cliff edge at the water miles and miles below.

The Forth Railway Bridge never seems to lose its fascination. In many ways it and its modern neighbour the new Road Bridge complement each other, being sufficiently far apart for this aspect to be appreciated—a situation which unfortunately could not be possible at Saltash over the Tamar, which divides Cornwall from "England", where the new road bridge had perforce to be built side by side with Brunel's masterpiece.

On contemplating over sixty different examples of the Forth Bridge in my picture postcard collection it occurred to me that it will soon be the centenary of its inception, and that a book on its building and successful completion would in fact be a microcosm of industrial engineering and the dynamic growth of heavy industry of the Victorians.

Lord Macaulay wrote in his essay on Clive of India that every schoolboy knew who strangled Atahualpa. This seems doubtful, but what is certain is that by the end of the nineteenth century and the first quarter of the next every schoolboy knew that there were at least 6½ million rivets employed in the construction of the Forth Bridge and that it took 3 years to paint, by which time it was time to start all over again.

Anthony Murray
Edinburgh, 1983.

1

BEFORE THE BRIDGE

The Queen's Ferry

Returning to his own country from the battle, the painted king, Hungus, crossed the sea at narrows of Inch Garvie; paused on the island there to impale the head of his foe upon a stake, where it remained for many years as a solemn warning to any who might venture North of the Forth, into the Kingdom of the Picts.
(Adapted from the Fourteenth Century *Scotti Chronicum* by John Forden)

Hungus was a King of the Picts in Fife at the dawn of history. His foe was the southern invader, Athelstane, and the battle was at Athelstaneford. The historical truth of the account is open to doubt, but what is certain is that, from time immemorial, there has been a ferry across the Firth of Forth at the point at which the Railway Bridge now stands.

Not a metalled road or a bridge, of course—everybody thought that was impossible until The Great Bridge was built—but a crossing point or a ferry linking the South to the fat farmlands of Fife and the old Scottish capital of Dunfermline. From about the time of the Norman conquest the ferry was known as the Queen's Ferry, after Malcolm Canmore's sainted Consort. Queen Margaret used the crossing regularly on her journeys to the shrine of St. Andrew in Fife, and, following

her example it became a well-worn pilgrim's path, where before it had been principally used for trade.

In 1123 Queen Margaret's son, Alexander I, was stormbound on the island of Inchcolm, downstream from the Inchgarvie narrows, while he was crossing the Forth "on business of State". He had narrowly escaped with his life, and might yet have perished on the tiny island had it not been for the food and shelter given to him by a hermit who lived there. In thanksgiving for his deliverance the King vowed to build a monastery on the island, but he died in the following year and it was left to his successor, David I, to carry out his vow. Possibly because of his predecessor's misfortune, David I took steps towards establishing a regular ferry across the Inchgarvie narrows, bestowing the right to control it upon the monks of Dunfermline.

The monks successfully ran the Queen's Ferry throughout medieval times and at the Reformation it became part of the lordship of Dunfermline. Then, in 1589, James VI gave the ferry rights to his bride as a wedding present, and shortly after this, early in the next century, the passage was divided notionally into sixteen parts which could be feued to individuals. This sixteen-part division remained in operation right down to the eighteenth century and those who controlled the feus, the feudal superiors, had the right to put boats on the Forth and provide the ferry service—a very lucrative business.

The superiors did not, of course, run the ferries themselves: the sloops and skiffs were operated by the ferrymen of North Queensferry, a proud community who regarded their job as a right and refused to allow outsiders to work the boats. They claimed that they had been settled in North Queensferry by Queen Margaret herself, and they certainly ran the boats for the monks of Dunfermline long before the sixteen-part division was made in the seventeenth century. They incurred Cromwell's wrath a hundred years later for adhering to the Catholic faith of their former master, even after the Reformation. They had a reputation for being quarrelsome and surly to outsiders: in 1637 two of the ferrymen, George Binks and John Blair, had to appear before the bailies of Dunfermline for "Injuring one another". They were fined five pounds each, the money to be paid not to the court but one to the other, and ordered that: "Ye said persons to end in friendship and to drink togedder and ye said George Binks to drink first to ye said John Blair in respect he did ye greatest violence to ye said John Blair yan ye said John Blair did to him". In the same year five boatmen were sent to jail for not taking the Lord of Doune across the river, and in the same decade the King himself, Charles I, having lost "Thirty-five of His Servantes, His siller, and hoosehold goodes" during a crossing, laid charges before the Privy Council accusing the ferrymen of "practices that tended more to their own lucre than to our subjects good and saftie".

In these days, fares were based on the quality of the passenger:

> Ilk duke, earl or viscount three shillings and four pence; ilk lord one shilling and four pence; any yr under ye degree for ye man or woman one penny; ilk horse, cow or ox two pennies; ilk twenty sheep four pennies.

One wonders what King Charles had to pay for his passage. The money collected in fares was split up among the community of ferrymen, after the owners of the feus had taken their rent (one-quarter of the takings) and after the "ferry silver" for maintaining the quays (one-fortieth of the total) had been paid. The whole sum available to the community at the end of the week was then divided up into "deals" or shares, according to the number of people entitled to a portion. Saturday night was when they were dealt out: one full deal to every man who had worked the boats; one half deal to every "retired" ferryman; a portion of a deal to any boys who worked, according to their age; even something for the widows of ferrymen and a sum for the teacher employed by the community to teach their children.

The importance of the Queen's Ferry is shown by the number of parliamentary statutes that were devoted to it, both before and after the Union of the Parliaments in 1707—"An Act that Ferriers mak Brigges and of Fraught" in the reign of James III, for example, or "How Meikle Fraught shall be given to Ferriers" in the reign of Queen Mary—and in spite of continual complaints the Passage seems to have been well serviced up to the middle of the eighteenth century, when several factors contributed towards it being adversely highlighted. Twice during the century, in 1745 and in 1779, the link with Fife was dramatically threatened, and on both these occasions its fragility was forcefully driven home. In 1745 all the ferryboats were destroyed by loyalists, who were terrified that they would be used by the victorious Jacobite army to reach Edinburgh; and in 1779 the pirate adventurer, Paul Jones, set up a base in the Forth and proceeded to terrorise shipping. To defend the ferry on this occasion four 24-pounder cannons were installed on Inchgarvie. They were never used, though, as the ferrymen preferred to stay at home while Mr. Jones was about.

Even without these dramatic events to draw attention to it, the Passage was notorious amongst eighteenth-century travellers and was much criticised. The age expected a more efficient service than previous times had, and a report at the turn of the century summed up what had been felt for many years: "The condition and situation of the ferry . . . cannot be described so far as to give an adequate idea of its defects": the shipping and landing places were "in every way inconvenient and dangerous"; the piers were few, "ill constructed and so placed as to give no facility in crossing when the wind and tide were unfavourable to a direct passage"; the service was irregular and "there was no system of regulation for the right conduct of the ferry, nor any superintendent to control it"; the ferrymen were as rude as ever and "their insubordination was a cause of just complaint". The boats were kept on the north side of the river, where the boatmen lived, and passengers often had to spend several hours, sometimes days if the weather turned bad, in the Hawes Inn at South Queensferry, waiting for a boat to come over.

Added to this was the problem of uncertain coach services from Edinburgh and non-existent services in Fife, although chaises were kept for hire at some villages. A contemporary joke about the situation was made by Sir Walter Scott in the opening chapter of *The Antiquary*, where the hero has waited in the coach office in Edinburgh until his patience has worn thin. He summons the person in charge:

> "Woman, is that advertisement thine", he cried . . . "and does it not set forth that, God willing, as you hypocritically express it, the Hawes Fly, or Queensferry Diligence, would set forth today at Twelve o'clock; and is it not, thou falsest of creatures, now a quarter past Twelve, and no such fly or diligence to be seen?"

The Antiquary railed on, finally demanding of the woman whether the coach existed at all:

> "Oh, dear yes," replied the harassed woman, "the neighbours ken the diligence weel—green picked out wi' red; three yellow wheels and a black ane."

The coach finally arrived and having paid his three shillings the Antiquary set off. Still the journey was not without mishap, however, for one of the horses cast a shoe and a spring broke on the coach, so that they missed the tide and the Antiquary and his companion were delayed and dined at the Hawes Inn while waiting for the boat. He arrived at Arbroath (or Fairport as it is called in the book), a distance of only sixty-seven miles, twenty-six hours after he had set out. This was the usual expectancy, and there was a saying that even with his own horse a traveller would breakfast at North Queensferry and eat his evening meal in Edinburgh.

A further factor that urged change was the considerable growth in traffic. By the beginning of the nineteenth century it was averred before a Parliamentary committee that unlicenced outsiders offering ferry services were making £5,000 per annum: the total rent payable by the ferrymen at this time was £2,000. In 1811 the number of passengers on the official ferries averaged 228 a day, rising to 447 a day during the busiest time of the year. In 1807 a Board of Trustees was set up to examine the condition of the ferry. They reported that:

> This Passage or Ferry, thought the most important and the most resorted to of any in the kingdom, is the property of private individuals, who, with all the good intentions possible, cannot be supposed likely to devote themselves to those considerations of public convenience and accommodation which the nature of the case requires.

They recommended that the service be "nationalised" and controlled by a Board of

Trustees, and a Bill was lodged in Parliament to that effect. The old heritable proprietors of the ferry were furious:

> Decidedly hostile to all provisions of the Bill. The unlimited authority granted to the Trustees would . . . cause irreparable injury to

the proprietors, and would constitute . . . a violent invasion of private property: a serious and alarming evil.

But in spite of this, the Bill received Royal Assent on May 20th 1809.

'One For Comers: One For Goers'

While these efforts were being made to improve the ferry service a group of engineers in Edinburgh were considering a different, indeed revolutionary, way of overcoming the problem of the Passage: a tunnel.

The daring scheme was typical of the times; a product of minds stimulated by "The Enlightenment" which swept Scotland, and particularly Edinburgh, in the closing decades of the eighteenth century. In 1804 work began on a tunnel under the Thames at Rotherhithe in the East End of London and, as one of the proposers of the Forth tunnel project said in reference to contemporary coal mining:

> At Borrowstoneness [i.e. Bo'ness] they have carried their workings under the same frith for a mile without experiencing any inconvenience. At Whitehaven they now work coal for about the same distance under the Irish sea, and at both places less water is met with in the workings under the sea than in workings under the land.

The moving force behind the scheme was John Grieve, an Edinburgh man. With two colleagues, William Vazie and James Taylor, he surveyed the bed of the Forth at Queensferry in 1805 and said: "I have no difficulty in saying that the thing is very practicable."

Practicable it may have been, but not easy. At the Inchgarvie narrows the river was very

deep, so excavations for the tunnel would have to be that much deeper; also a rib of hard whinstone ran out a part of the way from the south shore and this would make tunnelling difficult. They investigated further upstream and found a limestone bank to the west of Rosyth Castle on the north shore which would block tunnelling at that point. So the only suitable place was a small stretch between Rosyth and Inchgarvie, and this meant that the southern entrance to the tunnel would be close to Hopetoun House, a contingency hotly objected to by the Earl Hopetoun, who owned both the house and the land nearby. The Earl also objected to the steam-pumping engines that would be housed at the entrance to the tunnel while excavation was under way. He objected to the houses and offices that would require to be built. He objected to the camp that would be needed for the navvies. The indefatigable Grieve met all his objections, even, somewhat facetiously, tempting him with views of "a neat town at Rosyth, with the castle at its bosom, [which] would not detract from the scenery of Hopetoun House; but if the noble Earl thinks otherwise, he has that in his power."

Grieve's tunnel was estimated to cost about £160,000. It would take four years to complete. It was designed to be in two passages, "One for comers: one for goers" as he quaintly put it, each fifteen-feet high and fifteen-feet wide, with room for pedestrians on a raised sidewalk as well as the carriageway. The *Scots Magazine* of July 1806 pronounced it "a work in the highest degree curious and important", a prospectus was issued offering shares at £100 each, and there the matter rested. A further attempt to raise capital was made the following year, in conjunction with a pamphlet, *Observations on the Advantages and Practicability of Making Tunnels under navigable rivers, applicable to the proposed tunnel under the frith of Forth,* but still they were unsuccessful, and the scheme vanished into history.

Proposals for an Invisible Bridge

It [i.e. the Passage] *must be brought, if not to the state of perfection, as near to it as the nature of the thing will admit. The most perfect passage over a deep and broad water is a bridge which permits of passage at all moments. Where the water is so broad as not to admit of a bridge the very incapacity of applying a bridge renders it necessary to make the passage by vessels most perfect.*
(Letter from William Adam M.P. to Lord Primrose, one of the proprietors of the Queensferry Passage)

The above letter was written in 1808, and in assuming that the Forth could never be bridged Mr Adam did not sufficiently take into account the enterprise of the times. It was the age in which roads and bridges were appearing all over Scotland, opening up areas previously inaccessible to wheeled traffic. The times of Thomas Telford, the Rennie family and John Loudon McAdam. Times in which it seemed that the engineer might overcome all natural obstacles.

John Anderson, himself a Civil Engineer in Edinburgh, will have been aware of all these exciting developments, but his inspiration came primarily from the great wooden bridges of China that he had read about, some of them thousands of feet long; one even reputed to stretch three miles; one "connecting the tops of two mountains and thrown over a frightful valley of 750 feet in height". His bridge was to be the greatest in all the land, indeed it was to be one of the wonders of the modern world, a meeting of science and art; it was to be built at the old crossing place, the Inchgarvie narrows. He wrote:

The appearance and situation are altogether so favourable and so inviting for some work of art that it has often occurred to the reporter when he considered them attentively that a bridge of some description ought to be attempted.

The mile-and-a-half across the narrows was to be spanned in three great leaps, broken by two pillars, one at the edge of the shelf, before the river deepened, the other on Inchgarvie island. The pillars, or abutments, were to be cast-iron frames ninety feet tall, the iron to be dipped in linseed oil when hot to prevent rusting, and on top of these, vast iron columns would soar a further hundred feet. The roadway itself was to be suspended from numerous chains 90 or 110 feet (he submitted alternative plans) above the surface of the sea at high-tide, and it was to be made of the best materials—oak from America, iron from

Sweden, freestone from Well Dean Quarry near North Queensferry, lime from Elgin Limeworks.

The height of the roadway had been dictated by the height of the highest mast on the biggest vessel likely to use the Forth: the dimensions of the carriageway would provide ample room for wheeled traffic and pedestrians: twenty-five feet wide with four-foot sidewalks, or enough room for two loaded hay carts to pass one another and leave room for a stout pedestrian on either side. The abutments on which the structure rested were to be designed "to resemble in a certain degree the formation of rock" and the whole creation was "to be treated in a most artistic manner". And the time it would take to build? And the cost? And the quantity of materials?

Like Grieve's tunnel the bridge should be completed in four years (the railway bridge took seven years, 65 years later); the simplest of the three designs would cost only £144,000,

and this allowed £13,442 for contingencies (the railway bridge cost 3½ million pounds). To achieve the most artistic effect, the bridge was to be incredibly light—only 2,000-2,500 tons of iron would be required (the railway bridge used 52,000 tons of steel and, according to which report is believed, somewhere between 6½ million and 10 million rivets!) A later commentator dryly remarked that "the bridge would no doubt have presented a very light and slender appearance, so light, in fact, that on a dull day it would have been hardly visible, and after a severe gale it might have been no longer seen, even on a clear day".

Anderson expected support for the scheme from the Ferry Trustees, the Post Office and the City of Edinburgh, but the latter were too preoccupied with providing the town with a public water supply and street lighting, and the plan disappeared in the same way that schemes for Grieve's tunnel faded away.

Steam and Competition

Mister McAndrew, don't you think steam spoils romance at sea?
Rudyard Kipling, *McAndrew's Hymn*

The reaction of the Queensferry Passage Trustees to Mr. Anderson's chain bridge scheme is unfortunately not recorded, but it was clear to them by 1820, when the ferry first started to lose money, that something would have to be done. Admiral Sir Philip Durham, retired from the East India Company, warned that "a steamship could never live on the Forth" five years before, but in spite of this, by 1820 there were several steamers plying regularly about the Firth of Forth. This provided a further problem for

the unfortunate Trustees, for two of the steamers began to call at Kirkcaldy in Fife on their daily passage from Leith to Grangemouth, and others were quick to offer the more reliable steamer service to those trying to reach Fife. They would have to try a steamer themselves, and this they did, hiring the *Lady of the Lake* to see if steam could operate in the narrows. It worked well, and in 1821 the Trustees commissioned a vessel that would suit the Queensferry piers and quays and named her *Queen Margaret*.

This was a marked improvement on the sailing ships used previously and in 1828, after improvements had been made to the quays by Thomas Telford, the Trustees could report:

The transit at low water was made certain and excellent; the shipping and landing places convenient and safe; the regulations calculated to establish right conduct at the ferry . . . all extraneous traffic having been removed from the piers, there is no longer any interruption at the quays, or any embarrassment to embarking, disembarking, departing from the shore, approaching or landing at the piers.

But the Passage was still not without its risks. Ten years after that report was made there was an accident on the pier in which two passengers lost their lives when the lead horse of the coach collecting them turned its head and caused the coach to roll over and tumble into the sea. *The Scotsman* reported that "the melancholy result is entirely attributable to the dangerous practice recently introduced of loading the coach on the quay instead of at the Inn, as formerly, and at the same time leaving the horses heads unattended".

The Passage was also by no means clear of its difficulties. Although it was more reliable than previously, there was still a long trek to be made to or from South Queensferry and the ferry boat itself, which had never been fast, had now absorbed so much water that she settled low and was reckoned to be the slowest craft on the Forth. Worst of all, in 1818 a new pier, the Chain Pier, was opened at Newhaven by Edinburgh to augment the old service from Leith and to run ferries thence to Burntisland in Fife.

There had been a ferry from Leith for many years, known as the Broad Ferry and running two sloops, manned by four men each, on every tide. It sailed to Burntisland and Kinghorn, and later to Pettycur. It was from Pettycur that Dr. Thomas Guthrie, the famous preacher and philanthropist, sailed in 1815 to begin his studies at Edinburgh University (at the age of twelve—not an unusual age to start university in those days). It was a wet, blustery evening when he arrived at the ferry with his tutor, having walked the last ten miles to Pettycur, because of the lack of public transport in Fife. The boatmen refused to take the boat out for only two passengers, but at last the ferry superintendent ordered them out and they were joined by a woman passenger. They were no sooner out in the Firth than the crew tried to extort money out of the unfortunate Guthrie and his tutor, saying that if they didn't pay twice the fare they would pitch them overboard. They were saved in the end by the third passenger who silenced the crew with a fishwife's tongue, and they arrived safely in Leith.

In spite of its inadequacies and the longer sea passage, the Broad Ferry continued to steal trade from Queensferry, and when, in 1837, work was begun on a new and commodious harbour at Granton, with a broad approach road from the centre of Edinburgh, the situation looked grim for the Passage's Trustees and the, by now ageing, steamer that plied the narrows and which they could not afford to replace. Granton pier was opened by the brother of the Duke of Buccleuch, who had financed the project, on 28th June 1838, the day of Queen Victoria's coronation. *The Times* correspondent remarked:

I had repeatedly heard of this stupendous undertaking, its eligible situation, the facilities it afforded for the accommodation of passengers, goods, horses and carriages, embarking and disembarking, and the depth of water affording vessels at all times of the tide to approach it without danger, thereby avoiding that great inconvenience formerly experienced by passengers by the hazardous employment of small boats. . . . Can sufficient praise be bestowed on the noble founder of this great work, which, in a commercial point of view, will not only immortalise his name, but be the means of increasing to a great extent the trade of Edinburgh and its vicinity? . . . The whole seemed to be conducted with the greatest order and regularity, and that intolerable nuisance of porters, coachmen, cabmen and other vagrants was altogether avoided.

But in spite of what the correspondent says,

it seems that "vagrants" were not long kept away. Shortly after the opening, the Duke levied a toll of tuppence on every pedestrian using the new pier. Having just paid his due, a traveller who was accosted by a beggar protested that he had just given his last penny to the Duke of Buccleuch. "What"? said the vagrant, "is he upon the tramp too?"

To try and keep pace with the new Granton ferry service the Queensferry Trustees promoted an Act for the improvement of the landing stages at Queensferry in the same Coronation year, 1838. But by this time attention was being focused on the new railways, and it was clear that whoever gained a railway link first would secure the trade.

Railway Mania: Private Railway Companies in Scotland

Railway Shares! Railway Shares!
Hunted by Stags and Bulls and Bears—
Hunted by women—hounded by men—
Speaking and writing—voice and pen—
Claiming and coaxing—prayers and
  snares—
See the world mad about Railway
  Shares—
from *Illustrated London News*, 1845

In these times of a unified and nationalised railway system it is difficult for us to conceive of the fierceness of the competition between the hundreds of small railway companies that sprang up during the 1840s—an era that quickly became known as that of "Railway Mania"—and the keen interest that was shown by the public at large in the fortunes of railway schemes. Contemporary writers regarded the struggle to secure routes and build lines as a war between the companies. The term is not misapplied: in one year, 1846, no less than 1,263 bills were presented in Parliament seeking authority to build railways.

Like everywhere else, battles were fought to secure the routes in the East of Scotland: a fight for the line north of Perth, a long and acrimonious struggle for the Edinburgh-Glasgow line, a battle for the Kingdom of Fife and for the east coast route to Aberdeen. The "problem" of the railways in Scotland was compounded by the fact that all traffic was confined to the central belt and Aberdeenshire, with a line running to Ayr and one to Fife and Forfar: what remained of the traffic in Scotland consisted of, in the words of W.M. Acworth (*Scottish Railways*, 1890), "fish, flesh and fowl (or at least grouse), for the good red herring mostly goes by sea", and was hardly worth fighting for. Nevertheless the fight was fierce: indeed the restricted routes in Scotland led to a ferocity of competition equal to any in the railway world. France and Germany both had sluggish monopolies, and even in Lancashire there was such a thing as "non-competitive traffic". In Scotland there was practically none. As Acworth commented: "It is, then, in universal and ubiquitous competition that the keynote to the Scottish Railway System is to be found."

One of the earliest theatres of war was the fight for a railway line between Edinburgh and its port of Leith. Plans for a line connecting the two and running on to Newhaven—the first passenger project for an Edinburgh to Fife railway—was incorporated as the Edinburgh, Leith and Newhaven

Railway in 1836. As the *Railway Record* of the time remarked, "probably there is no instance on record of a railway company having encountered so many difficulties . . . and living". In this case the difficulties were not so much attributable to competition from other companies as to massive claims for compensation from owners of property over, or under, which the line passed, and to the loss of faith of the shareholders.

The proposed line was to run from Princes Street to Trinity Pier, a distance of about 2¼ miles. A contemporary observer commented that "among the excavations in Edinburgh, none could appear more extraordinary than the formation of a tunnel from the old locality of Canal Street to Scotland Street", but this was actually accomplished after laborious and expensive engineering. The terminus at Edinburgh consisted of a dingy shed and a couple of platforms situated at Canal Street, at the East End of Princes Street, at right angles to the combined North British and Edinburgh & Glasgow station. Leaving the station, the line ran for a thousand yards under the New Town, down a gradient of one in twenty-seven, to Scotland Street. The company's prospectus mentioned the use of locomotives which "must consume their own smoke", but the incline proved to be too severe for steam haulage and so a stationary engine and ropes were used. The trains left Canal Street every fifteen minutes, careering down the tunnel by gravity. Each train was headed by a couple of special brake trucks, manned by brakesmen, who held the train in check, but the screeching noise of the brake-blocks against the wheels, combined with flying sparks and general clatter, made the short trip a terrifying one for those of nervous disposition.

In the end it took six years to link the capital with Newhaven, by which time it was necessary to continue the line to the new harbour built by the Duke of Buccleuch "with £80,000 out of his own pocket", at Granton.

This was finally reached in 1846, and the link with Leith was completed in the same year, the company having changed its name to the Edinburgh, Leith and Granton Railway in 1842.

At this time the ease with which freight could be brought to Granton—coal especially —gave the Broad Ferry considerable advantage over the struggling Queensferry, an advantage which had been consolidated when, in 1842, improvements were made to Burntisland harbour by the Duke of Buccleuch and Sir John Gladstone (W.E. Gladstone's father). The construction of railway lines in Fife, finally secured in 1847 after three years of hard fighting by the Edinburgh and Northern Railway Company, also helped.

The 1840s, then, set the pattern for the railway system which was to evolve in Scotland. The Edinburgh & Northern Company absorbed the Edinburgh, Leith & Granton, and also purchased the Burntisland to Granton Ferry in 1847, and the parent company then changed its name to the Edinburgh, Perth & Dundee Railway in 1849. The 1840s, though, also saw the growth of a company which, in 1862, would take over even the new Edinburgh, Perth and Dundee Railway Company. The North British Railway was incorporated on 19th July, 1844, for the construction of a line from Edinburgh to Berwick, with a branch to Haddington. The 46-mile line was opened in June two years later, and during the ensuing seventy years the North British was to become one of the two great forces in the Scottish railway system, taking over some fifty independent railway companies and control of the Union Canal between Edinburgh and Falkirk as well as the Forth and Tay ferry systems.

It was also developments in the 1840s which led to the recruitment by the Edinburgh and Northern railway of a young engineer of vision and energy. Thomas Bouch was only twenty-six when he was appointed manager and chief engineer with a brief to advise a way of making the ferry service more efficient. He had worked as a railway engineer since he was seventeen, and for the previous four years had been one of the resident engineers on the pioneer Stockton and Darlington Railway. He also laid out a tramway system in Edinburgh and was obsessed with ideas for overcoming the great water breaks of Forth and Tay, and within a year of his appointment he was pressing the directors with a plan for ferries which could be used for carrying railway vehicles across both estuaries.

The main problem was to overcome the formidable twenty-foot difference between high and low tide on the rivers. Bouch ingeniously got round this by designing a sixty-foot long platform mounted on rails on the harbour slipway with a thirty-five-foot ramp attached to its seaward end with universal joints which would compensate for the height of the tide in loading the ferry. The whole device was designed to be level with the deck of the ferry at half-tide, and thus at high and low water the slope would be minimised. The ferry-boat itself was driven by two enormous and independently operated paddle wheels which rose up on either side of the low deck, on which stood the railway trucks—not the engines; they remained on the quayside.

In January 1850 the first train ferry in the world, named the *Leviathan* and built especially for the run, was ready for trials. The directors of the Edinburgh, Perth and Dundee Railway saw twelve trucks loaded in seven minutes at Burntisland, and then themselves crossed with the ferry in twenty-five minutes (the only time a passenger coach was to be carried over on the ferry), and watched the ship unload in three minutes before adjourning to the Granton Hotel for lunch.

The *Leviathan* was a great success and another vessel was soon ordered to serve the Tay. In the next decade passenger services were introduced from a separate pier, although for some reason the carriages themselves were not transported, and right up to the opening of the Forth Bridge passengers had to disembark, walk down the slipway and endure the often very uncomfortable passage in the open. Consider, then, a journey from Edinburgh to Dundee in, say, 1860.

Prior to leaving, the traveller would consult his waistcoat-pocket sized *Murray's Diary*, first published in the 1840s and an institution for Edinburgh citizens until it ceased publication in 1966. This was a comprehensive local timetable, and invariably had a small sheet of Ford's blotting paper bound into it among the other advertisements: its alphabetical list of destinations, with train times and fares in clear columns were a godsend to those who would have been floored by Bradshaw, the famous complete national timetable. From *Murray's* the traveller would find that the cab fare from the south side of the city, where we shall assume him to be living, was 1/6d to the North Bridge Stations (there was a chaotic clutch of stations on the site of the present Waverley Station), and that the cabby must help to load and unload the luggage. The fare to Dundee was 8/6d First Class, down to 4/1½d Fourth Class. Trains left at 6.00a.m., 9.30a.m., 2.00p.m. and 6.00p.m.

He would leave North Bridge by Canal Street Station (sometimes called Princes Street Station) on a train which ran by gravity through a tunnel under the New Town to Scotland Street Station, a journey of three minutes. There he would change to steam haulage and continue to Granton, reaching the port in about twelve minutes. The vehicle he would be travelling in would have had no heating of any sort and so our traveller will have been laden down with travelling rugs and a good heavy coat, perhaps with a flask of spirits in its pocket, if he was journeying during the winter months. Scrambling out of the train he hurries down the slippery cobbles of Granton pier, holding onto his hat with one hand and to his rugs and luggage with the other. If he had left the Capital in order to reach Dundee as early in the day as possible, he would have departed from Canal Street at 6.00a.m. in order to catch the ferry leaving Granton at 6.20.

The shallow-draught ferry offered no shelter to its sorry passengers, who had to find what space they could amongst the clutter of boxes, carts and other paraphernalia on the flat deck. The passage journey did not last long, however, and if there were no delays, the passenger would arrive at Burntisland in about half-an-hour. After walking the long haul up to the station, he would then board the 7.00a.m. train for Tayport, where the ferry

procedure was repeated and Dundee finally reached about 9.00 a.m.

The three-and-a-half hours it took to travel the fifty miles between Edinburgh and Dundee was a great improvement on the two days it took prior to the introduction of the ferry service and the rail links. There was no doubt in the minds of the Boards of the railway companies however, that ferries could not offer serious competition for the main route North so long as the journey was so broken up: bridges across both rivers would be the only thing that would improve the service. But was this possible?

Bouch's train ferry for the Firth of Forth between Granton and Burntisland in 1850.

2

THE IMPOSSIBLE DREAM

Thomas Bouch's Floating Bridge

Without running the risk of involving ourselves in the presumption of those who take upon them to set boundaries and limits to the possible achievements of science, it may be admitted that in all likelihood, for many years to come, no very considerable improvements can be effected in the rate of quickness at which the railways' boats are now taken across the ferries.

(James Bruce: *Tullis's Guide to the Edinburgh and Northern Railway*)

Thomas Bouch's obsession with the problem of crossing the Forth and Tay estuaries was not diminished by the introduction of the floating ferry. Indeed, only three years after its opening he had approached his employers with an outline plan for a bridge across the Tay: he was turned down flatly, being told "that it was the most insane idea that could ever be propounded". Shortly after this Bouch left the Edinburgh, Perth and Dundee Railway Company and set up his own consultancy firm, to work on, amongst other things, proposed rail connections to Fife.

The principal reason for the revival of the Old Passage was the developing competition between the North British Railway Company of the East Coast and the Edinburgh and Glasgow Railway, allied to the Caledonian Railway Company, on the West Coast. Both wanted to expand North and, in pursuance of this the North British went on to negotiate an amalgamation with the Edinburgh, Perth and Dundee Railway, which gave them control of the whole of Fife, and finally, in 1863, an amalgamation with the Edinburgh and Glasgow itself secured the connection with the West. *The Railway Times* called the amalgamation of the two old enemies "a natural and unimpeachable alliance": it effectively left the North British as the power in Central and South-East Scotland and, as such, the principal opponent to the Caledonian Railway which controlled the South-West, for the route North. As both sides manoeuvred for the most important battle of the Northern railway wars it became clear to the directors of the North British that victory would be theirs only if they could improve the links with Fife and Angus, and this meant bridges.

As early as 1860-61 Bouch had told the directors of the North British of his conviction that the rivers could be bridged, but at that time the Board had been sceptical. After the amalgamation their attitude was different and they instructed him to draw up plans.

He thought the Queensferry Passage too deep to bridge and chose a site five miles upstream, between Blackness on the southern shore and Charlestown in Fife. The problem here was that the river-bed did not afford secure foundation for the piers that would support the structure, being composed of mud to a depth of about 200 feet below the river's bottom. The confident Bouch would not hear the word impossible, however, and devised a scheme for a lattice-girder bridge, 150 feet above the surface of the water and two miles long, which would be supported by 61 stone piers resting in the mud. He believed that the weight of the super-structure would compress the mud to an extent that would prohibit movement of the piers: in effect the pier would be "floating" in the mud.

Understandably, there were some who were not so convinced by the proposal, and an enquiry was held to investigate the plans: "You do admit that if the pressure of the wind operated so as to make one of these columns sink lower than the others, your bridge might come down?" asked Counsel at the Enquiry. "No, I do not even admit that." Throughout the meeting Bouch was supremely confident in his replies. "I had one of the columns of the Bala Bridge gone and there was no bridge came down or anything of that sort. I cannot suppose that under any possible circumstances this thing could happen . . ." Bouch won the day, and the North British was given Parliamentary permission to go ahead with the scheme. In June 1866 crowds watched a massive raft being launched at Burntisland and being towed up the Forth towards the Queensferry narrows. Working on top of this platform builders were to construct a stout brick tower, the shell for the first pier, which, once it had reached a certain height would be filled with 10,000 tons of iron so that it would sink and settle into the muddy river bed. Two tugs, moored alongside the raft, were provided for the builders to work from and live in.

In August they were about to sink the first pier when they were visited by a deputation of North British directors, including the Chairman of the Board who ordered that work stop immediately and dismissed the surprised builders there and then. The North British Railway Company was in grave financial difficulties, and in the shareholders' row that followed the annual report for that year it was stated that the accountancy system employed by the Company "was not merely one of general deception of the share-holders and misrepresentation of the company's affairs; it was not merely deliberate falsification of the accounts from year to year, so as to show to the shareholders and divide among them a revenue which was not in existence, but it was a careful and most ingenious fabrication of imaginary account, begun and carried on from time to time for the purpose of supporting the falsified half-yearly statements of revenue and the general mis-representation of affairs!"

The Board was removed and the pugnacious John Stirling of Kippendavie appointed chairman to put the company back on its feet. For a time all plans for a bridge were shelved as being too costly, and improvements were undertaken to the jetties at Queensferry and to the ferry vessel there, the old *Willie Adam*, which was replaced, much to the annoyance of its supporters, by an unpopular screw-driven vessel, the first of its kind on the Forth. Some years later this steamer, the *John Beaumont*, sank after ramming the quay at North Queensferry. Her delighted critics advised the Board:

Directors o' the N.B.R.
You ne'er should try to lift her;
There's mony better boats by far—
The 'Willie' e'en was swifter.

You'll find that paddles beat the screw,
Although ye've sair misca'ed them;
And nane can wish a smarter crew
Than sailed the 'Willie Adam'.

Bouch's Tay Bridge and
New Plans for a Forth Bridge

Beautiful new railway bridge of the silvery
Tay,
With your strong brick piers and buttresses
in so grand array;
And your thirteen central girders, which
seems to my eye
Strong enough all windy storms to defy.
And as I gaze upon thee my heart feels
gay,
Because thou art the greatest railway
bridge of the present day;
And can be seen for miles away,
From north, south, east, or west, of the
Tay;
On a beautiful and clear sun shiny day,
And ought to make the hearts of the Mars
boys feel gay;
Because thine equal no where can be seen,
Only near by Dundee and the bonny
Magdalen Green.

(The first stanza of a poem, *An Address To The New Tay Bridge* by William McGonagall, composed 20th June, 1887. From a broadsheet in the author's collection.)

John Stirling knew that the success of the North British in their war with the Caledonian Railway would, in the end, depend on bridging the Forth and Tay estuaries, and, in September 1869, soon after he became chairman, he travelled to Dundee to meet the town council and harbour trustees to persuade them to lend financial support to a bridge across the Tay.

The proposed bridge was designed by Thomas Bouch, who accompanied Stirling, and who had himself lobbied the idea for a bridge at a public meeting in Dundee in 1864. On that occasion he had said: "It is a very ordinary undertaking, and we have several far more stupendous and greater bridges already constructed . . . I have estimated the cost at £180,000, and I will stake my professional reputation that the cost will not exceed this amount." Rash words, for the final cost was £350,000, but at the time Bouch's claims and his showmanship raised rapturous applause, and when James Cox, one of the richest men in Dundee and later the city's Lord Provost, said that he would invest in the project the meeting agreed that "it would be for the public advantage, and lend greatly to the traffic of the North of Scotland and especially to the town and trade of Dundee."

Numerous difficulties were encountered in the construction of the bridge and progress was very slow, but at last the job was done and Major General Hutchinson, the government inspector, came up from London to examine the stupendous work of engineering. He undertook various tests over the course of three days, running loads over the bridge far heavier than it would have to carry and carefully examining the piers and super-structure. In his report he pronounced himself satisfied that the bridge was sound for passenger traffic, although he qualified this by saying that there should be a speed limit and adding, "I should wish if possible to have an opportunity of observing the effects of a high wind when a train of carriages is running over the bridge". This last statement was to prove crucial in the months to come, and the fact that Hutchinson had written it saved his skin. The Tay Bridge was opened in March 1878, "with as much éclat as possible" and 1500 people crossed the bridge to meet thousands of

Dundonians on the Angus side. Stirling and Bouch were given the freedom of the City of Dundee. The papers called it "the most stupendous bridge ever created". The Emperor of Brazil, after visiting the bridge, became convinced that a similar structure could be thrown across the Amazon. And, highest accolade of all, a year later Bouch was summoned to Windsor and knighted by the Queen.

Even before the Tay Bridge was complete, Bouch had again turned his attention to the Forth and, in 1873, re-drew his plans for a bridge which would this time avoid the use of "floating" columns. The second design was for a suspension bridge to be located at Queensferry and using Inchgarvie as the base for its central towers. The towers were to be 600 feet high and each of the spans, North and South from Inchgarvie, were to be 1600 feet long. From the immense steel towers two railway tracks, one hundred feet apart, were to be suspended by steel chains—rather like Grieve's "one for comers, one for goers" tunnel. The steel used was to be of "such tenacity that a load of ten tons per square inch could be safely carried", and the two tracks were to be "securely bound together with strong lateral bracing".

A company was formed to put the plan into operation—the Forth Bridge Railway Company—although Stirling cautiously sought the opinion of eminent experts about the plan and of the Astronomer Royal about doubts which had been expressed concerning the structure's capacity to withstand wind pressure. In their report, two of the experts, William Henry Barlow and William Pole, concluded that the design involved expensive materials and much complexity in the strains. Though their terms of reference did not include suggestions for an alternative design, they ventured to remark:

> From the great magnitude of parts, not only will inaccuracies in the manufacture or adjustment be more likely to creep in than in the works of smaller dimensions, but the mere changes of temperature during the manufacture and erection may, if not guarded against, produce important and unexpected inequalities in dimension, and corresponding variations in the strains.

They wished it to be understood that while they raised no objection to Bouch's system, "we do not commit ourselves to an opinion that it is the best possible". The Astronomer Royal, for his part, concluded that "with attention to these principles, and with due attention to the details of construction, I have no doubt of the perfect success of the Bridge, and I should be proud to have my name associated with such a noble enterprise". On 5th August, 1873, an act was obtained to allow work to commence.

The Forth Bridge Railway Company comprised the North British, the North Eastern, the Midland, and the Great Northern Railway Companies. These were East Coast lines from London with a vested interest in the success of the Bridge—the NBR would operate the trains whilst the FBR would maintain the structure.

For four years the project was held up due to lack of funding, and due to the North British's involvement on the Tay. Finally on the last day of September 1878 the foundation stone for a bridge across the Forth was laid by Mrs Bouch, and by the Spring of the following year the journal, *Engineering*, reported a "massive column of brickwork beginning to show itself on the western end of Inchgarvie". This lonely brick column, still to be seen in the Forth off Inchgarvie, is all that was ever completed of "this gigantic undertaking . . . the crowning triumph in Sir Thomas Bouch's distinguished professional career".

On the evening of 28th December 1879, during a violent gale, the Tay Bridge collapsed, taking with it a passenger train and seventy-three souls. The public outcry was

Top: "The Leviathan"—the first steamer conveying railway wagons across the Forth
Bottom: The ferry boat "Carrier"

The moveable cradle by which the railway wagons were run into
goods steamers at the ferry

unprecedented: were the engineering wonders of the age not to be trusted after all? Even before the public enquiry the following year, Bouch was the butt of public acrimony and by the end of the four-month investigation he was utterly discredited.

It was clear that wind pressure had not been adequately catered for in the bridge's construction, and during the enquiry Bouch himself made the extraordinary admission that no allowances had been made for exceptional wind pressure. It was calculated that the bracing ties on the bridge were less than half the strength necessary to withstand the maximum pressure that a cross-wind might be expected to exert on a train. This was by no means all. It transpired that Bouch had left the supervision of the building in the hands of the contractors, and they had delegated responsibility to the site agent, who had in his turn relied on the works foreman, Fergus Ferguson. Ferguson had authorised the covering up of defects in the cast-iron columns with a substance called Beaumontage (known in the trade as "Beaumont Egg"), made of beeswax, fiddler's rosin and iron filings, which, when smoothed with a hot iron and painted, invisibly filled cavities in the girders. Major cracks had appeared in the masonry of the piers and Bouch himself had given instructions that the columns be bound with iron bands. The river bed had been scoured by tidal flow at the base of some of the columns, and Bouch had instructed that the hollows be filled with loose stones. After the bridge opened, Bouch's assistant, Henry Noble, had been left in charge of maintenance but he had received no orders to report defects.

The wreck commissioner reported to the Committee of Inquiry:

> It is difficult to understand how the numerous defects should have been allowed to pass if there had been proper and competent persons to superintend the work . . . With the absence of all supervision we can hardly wonder that the columns were not cast so perfectly as they should have been.

The Report concluded that:

> The bridge was badly designed, badly constructed and badly maintained and that its downfall was due to inherent defects in the structure which must sooner or later have brought it down. For these defects both in design, construction and maintenance Sir Thomas Bouch is in our opinion mainly to blame.

During the four months of the enquiry the hair on Sir Thomas's head had turned white: at the end of it he was completely discredited as an engineer and as a man, and he died six months later in Moffat, Dumfriesshire, of "acute melancholia".

To Bridge Or Not To Bridge

We are not surprised that the project is given up. The Tay Bridge disaster was enough to strike terror into the hearts of ordinary shareholders in such an undertaking.
(*Herepath's Railway Journal*)

Until the Committee of Enquiry into the Tay Bridge Disaster had published their report work continued on Bouch's Forth Bridge. Application was made to the Board of Trade for permission to lower the bridge ten or fifteen feet; notices were served on Lord

Rosebery to take some of his land at South Queensferry and a field was pegged out for the construction of a railway siding and workshop; a brickworks was set up at Inverkeithing. There was a small inauguration ceremony which involved cutting a piece of turf and tipping a barrow-load of earth.

When the unequivocal blame for the Tay Bridge Disaster was laid on Sir Thomas Bouch, however, public and press were loud in their criticism of his Forth Bridge plan. His designs were checked again by experts, but it was the same team of experts as had checked the plans on the first occasion and the press considered that they would be biased in favour of them. Letters of protest were written to the papers and it was clear that there was a massive loss of faith in the project. Also, it was known that new and far more stringent regulations were to be introduced by the Board of Trade to control standards and specifications in engineering practice. So with great reluctance the Board of the Forth Bridge Railway Company abandoned the project, with the shareholders' support, on 13th January 1881, cancelling contracts and paying compensation where necessary. A formal Abandonment Bill was placed before Parliament.

The three English companies who had offered to guarantee an income to shareholders would not relinquish the lucrative connection with the North quite so simply, however. Matthew William Thompson, the chairman of the Midland Railway, called a meeting of representatives of the Boards of the Great Northern and the North Eastern Railways, in York early in 1881 and the feeling was that, while Bouch's plans would have to be shelved, a bridge of some sort might still be built. Each of the companies went away to consult their engineers, William H. Barlow for the Midland, Thomas Harrison for the North Eastern and Sir John Fowler for the Great Northern. Barlow and Harrison had been among the experts consulted previously,

so they were no strangers to the problems of bridging the Forth: Fowler, and his assistant, Benjamin Baker, had successfully constructed two major bridges across the Severn. After very thorough consideration of the situation— they even reopened the possibility of tunnelling—they concluded that a bridge was possible, though not a suspension bridge, and commenced preparation of detailed plans.

The Abandonment Bill had now passed the Commons and was awaiting consideration by the Lords. The Southern companies stepped in, guaranteed the shareholders an income of 4%, thus preventing the liquidation of the Forth Bridge Company, and recalled the Bill. On Friday, 30th September 1881, Fowler and Baker laid their plan for a new bridge before the chairmen and managers of the English companies and the North British. Harrison and Barlow, who had been kept closely informed about the progress their colleagues had been making, were enthusiastic about the plan, and within two hours it had been accepted by the railways and instructions given for the preparation of a new Parliamentary Bill. When the Bill came before Parliament, in the Spring of 1882, there was little opposition. The engineers whose design it was were, after all, the best in the country, and the government's inspectors had gone over the whole plan with Fowler and Baker. Also, a thirteen-foot model was laid before the House—and aroused so much interest that it was put on show there afterwards. The Bill received the Royal Assent on 12th July 1882.

The Act that authorised the building of a bridge across the Forth might be expected to have been hedged with constructional stipulations, born of the massive popular fears that had been aroused by the collapse of the Tay Bridge. This was certainly the case. Parliament imposed many restrictions, and, to make sure they were adhered to, instructed that the Board of Trade should inspect every stage of construction, reporting four times a year until the project was complete. The most

Old Waverley Bridge and Scotland Street
Tunnel Portal around 1850, from the Bank of
Scotland headquarters

important consideration was that the bridge "gain the confidence of the public and enjoy a reputation of being not only the biggest and strongest, but also the stiffest bridge in the world". The maximum amount of rigidity, both vertically under rolling load and horizontally under wind pressure, was to be obtained so that there would be no possibility of vibration. At every stage of construction the incomplete structure must be as secure as the finished article. Only the very best materials were to be used, the steel meeting the same rigorous requirements with Lloyds as that used in ship-building; and so on. And yet the "maximum amount of economies consistent with the fulfillment of the preceding conditions" were to be applied. The concern and caution of the engineers, combined with these restrictions resulted in the finished installation being at least twice as secure as it needed to be.

THE FORTH BRIDGE, CANTILEVER TYPE; ORIGINAL AND FINAL DESIGNS.

MESSRS. HARRISON, BARLOW, FOWLER, AND BAKER, ENGINEERS.

Fig. 4.

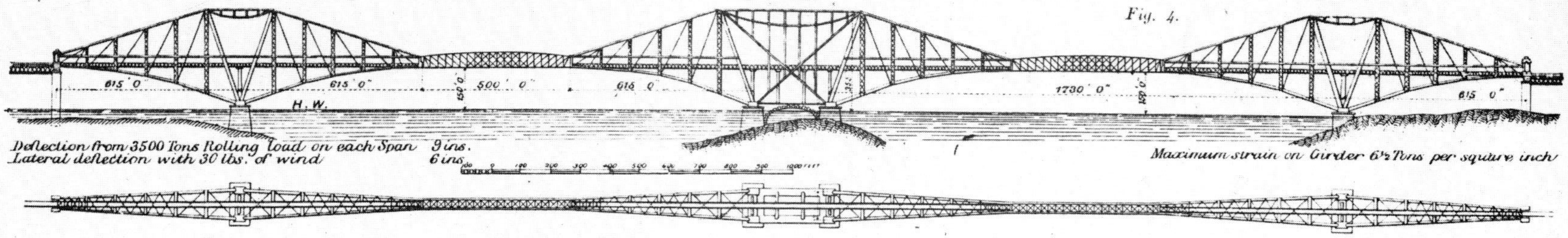

Deflection from 3500 Tons Rolling Load on each Span 9 ins.
Maximum strain on Girder 6½ Tons per square inch.
Lateral deflection with 30 lbs. of wind.

Fig. 5.

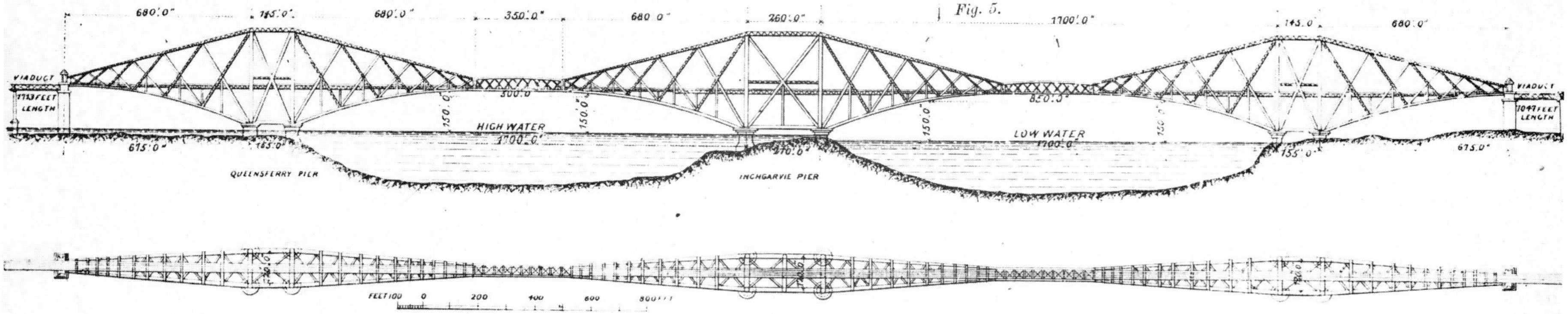

3

THE BIGGEST BRIDGE
IN THE WORLD

As it stands today, the bridge is a fitting monument to the engineering genius and scientific skill of the nineteenth century, and there is every likelihood that it will, for at least many years to come, rank as the first engineering wonder of the world.

(Frederick Stoton,
Bridging the Firth of Forth, 1910)

In the months following the passing of the Act, the design for the bridge which was to be the biggest in the world was eagerly taken up by the public and the press. Camps were formed for and against, the latter being led by the Astronomer Royal himself, who wrote in *The Times*: "We may reasonably expect the destruction of the Forth Bridge in a gale lighter than that which destroyed the Tay Bridge." Queues of spectators visited the model in the Houses of Parliament, and the designers of the marvel were continually asked to justify it, an important thing for them to be able to do, as in the end there would be no point in having a bridge that did not inspire confidence in those who were going to use it.

CANTILEVERS

In particular, Benjamin Baker was asked about his "novel" use of cantilevers. He explained that the term means no more than "bracket", and that an ordinary balcony or shelf is a form of cantilever. Originally he was not even happy about the term being applied to his bridge:

> When I was a student a girder bridge which had a top member in tension and the bottom member in compression over the piers was called a continuous girder bridge. The Forth Bridge is of that type, and I used to call it a continuous girder bridge; but the Americans persisted in calling all the bridges they were building on the same plan 'cantilever bridges'.

There was nothing novel in the design, even of cantilever bridges: bridges of this sort were being built in China, Tibet and India and from time immemorial, certainly before the birth of the English language.

In order to demonstrate the principle of the cantilever bridge more effectively he devised a human model, photographs of which were published in papers all over the world. In this illustration two men sat in chairs facing the camera, some three yards apart. With arms outstretched on either side they grasped the top ends of half-broomsticks, the bottoms of which were attached to their seats. The tops of the broomsticks between the men were connected by a short plank, while the tops furthest away were each anchored to piles of bricks.

The public were asked to imagine that the men's heads were the summits of the towers, 360 feet above the level of the river, their arms and the sticks were the cantilevers and

*Benjamin Baker's living model, demonstrating the principle of the
cantilever bridge*

A photograph dated May 1889 showing navvies, suitably posed for the occasion, on the Aberdour section. Anyone in brass buttons was usually a railway employee, whilst the others in this case belong to John Waddel the contractors. The clothing demarcation twixt the various working grades in those days was always very obvious. A bowler hat for instance atop overalls immediately proclaimed some authority, let alone a complete suit of clothes with golden albert.

There is no doubt that the best way to shift mountains is to organise hoards of men and arm them with picks and shovels. This is of course no longer possible, so, that even with vast modern pieces of earth-moving machinery it seems to take an unconscionable time to build a few miles of dual carriageway. Given the choice, in imagination, the Victorians would have settled for manpower and got on with it.

An official outing to the works, 1885

*Opposite Top: Outside Waverley Station at Princes Street
Gardens, around the time of the building of the Forth Bridge
Opposite Bottom: An old Edinburgh, Perth and Dundee Railway
goods engine, dating from the 1860s*

the plank in the middle was the central girder of the bridge. On the plank perched Kaichi Watanabe, a Japanese student of Messrs. Fowler & Baker, and a nice reference to the fact that the cantilever bridge had been invented in the East. When Kaichi sat on his plank the men's arms and the ropes to the bricks came under tension and the sticks and the chair-legs under compression: the one supported the other, and the whole structure was stable.

MATERIALS

In order to make the vast structure as light as possible the main compression members were to be made of tubes of steel plate 1¼ inches thick and twelve feet in diameter. Baker remarked that the weight they might have to support from trains overhead, wind, and their own deadweight (a total of 6,224 tons) was comparable to that of a contemporary transatlantic liner laden with cargo. The vertical tubes—the bodies of the men and the chair-legs—were made in a similar style, although the steel used here was not quite as thick. The main tubular members were to be connected with a latticework of steel girders. Such a mass of metal would be subject to considerable expansion in hot or cold weather and so each tube had special expansion joints built into it, which would allow for a variation of up to eighteen inches. This was more than twice the figure that had been calculated as the extreme possible variation.

All the steel used was to be top quality Siemans—some 52,000 tons would be required, braced together with some 6½ million rivets—and the larger plates and girders were to be cut and drilled on site. Other parts were moulded in the steel foundries of Glasgow, Motherwell and Swansea which provided material for the whole erection, and sent to Queensferry ready-made. In order to prepare the templates and patterns for the various parts of the construction an enormous loft was set up among the sheds and workshops of South Queensferry, with a blackened floor, upon which life-sized drawings of the parts could be made. The vast metal structure must rest on secure foundations, and here again only the best materials were used: fine Portland cement (over 21,000 tons) and Aberdeen granite (740,000 cubic feet) being the most important.

It is interesting to consider the tests that the cement had to undergo before it was deemed satisfactory. After being mixed with three times its weight of dry sand, the cement was required to be able to pass through a sieve of 400 meshes to the square inch, but to be retained by a sieve of 900 meshes, and when mixed with a proper proportion of water could be made into briquettes which could be able to withstand a tensile stress of 170 lbs per square inch of section without fracture, even after having been "kept in a damp atmosphere for 24 hours and then immersed in water for 28 days".

The construction contract was won by Messrs. Falkiner & Tancred of London and Messrs. Arrol of Glasgow. Both firms had wide experience of building bridges and William Arrol was no stranger to the Queensferry site, having started work on Bouch's abortive bridge three years previously. At the time that work started on the construction of the Forth Bridge Arrol was half way through building the new Tay Bridge.

WORKSHOPS AND SHEDS

Work officially commenced on 6th June 1883, with the laying of the first block in one of the piers for the approach viaduct by Sir Thomas Tancred, with full masonic honours. Offices and stores which had been erected by Arrol at North Queensferry in connection with Bouch's

Earthmoving machinery in its infancy, but mighty powerful. A steam navvy at work, probably one of Dunbar and Ruston's. Motor carriers instead of horse traction were still in the future.

bridge were pressed into service and added to, and as work progressed wooden huts were built for the workmen and their families, and later a canteen, stores, a dining-room and a reading-room were added.

The principal workshops were at South Queensferry. Here were built steel workshops and drill roads for assembling the steel plates; cement stores and timber yards; joiners' and carpenters' shops; a grocer's shop and a clothing and boot store; offices and pattern shops, including the drawing loft already mentioned. In addition there sprang up a small village of sixteen brick houses and forty wooden huts to accommodate part of the workforce, as well as "about sixty tenements in Queensferry for leading hands and gangers".

At South Queensferry the ground rises steeply from the shore and it was necessary to excavate and level the ground in terraces to accommodate the workshops. By the peak of the work on the bridge, the village and site covered sixty acres! Even on Inchgarvie buildings appeared: the old keep and battlements were roofed to provide "the most necessary shops and offices and stores", and later "a substantial cottage and kitchen, and sleeping accommodation for ninety foreign workmen" was built.

CAISSONS

Inchgarvie was the key to the whole enterprise. Without there being this small island in almost the middle of the Firth no cantilever bridge would have been possible. This was the firm base upon which the legs of the massive central "chair" would rest. Because of the immensity of the base, however, it was not possible to locate the legs on the dry land of the island itself: they must rise up from the sea-bed close by, in depths ranging from seventy-two to fifteen feet at high water.

Below the surface of the sea the legs were to be constructed of mass concrete: above water,

of granite blocks filled with rubble and cement. The problem immediately encountered by the contractors was to find a way of seating a "mould" into which the concrete could be poured firmly on the sea bed: to meet this problem submersible caissons were used. A caisson is a gigantic wrought-iron cylinder, not unlike a gasometer, seventy feet in diameter and between fifty and ninety feet high, depending on the depth they were sunk to. Empty they weighed about 500 tons: filled with concrete, between 4,000 and 20,000 tons. They were built sectionally in Glasgow, assembled in South Queensferry, towed out and sunk on the precise spot where the pier was to stand.

The bottom of each cylinder was equipped with a cutting edge and was shaped to the contours of the sea-bed at the place on which it would stand: before it was lowered a temporary layer of sandbags was laid on the bottom of the sea to give this edge something to bite on. The actual bottom of each caisson was set up seven feet above the cutting edge, so that, when the cylinder was settled onto the sea-bed, compressed air could be pumped into this space, creating a chamber of seventy feet in diameter and seven feet high for men to work in. Electric light was led down to the chamber and shafts ran through the solid body of the caisson connecting it to the surface and allowing access and egress for both men and materials. The men, many of whom were Italians (the contracting company for this work was French), could hack out and blast the rock away and settle the vast pier firmly into the rocky bed of the Firth.

Benjamin Baker remarked that many visitors came to look down into the lighted chamber far below, and W. Westhofen, who was in charge of work at Inchgarvie, mentions other visitors:

> Through gaps left in the heaps of sandbags a number of strange visitors used to make their appearance, attracted, no doubt, by the glare

A rather important-looking group of the age of the engineer on location

The approach viaduct near Inverkeithing. The line on the left is from Dunfermline to North Queensferry harbour, opened 1878.

of the lighted chamber. . . salmon, dogfish, octopus, many other fish, crabs and a large number of lobsters. One of the latter—a large specimen—got very excited in the chase after him and leapt up nearly the full height of the chamber, in his frantic endeavours to escape—finally jumping into an empty skip, whence he was promptly transferred to the boiling pot.

Hugh Douglas mentions a visitor who went down into the chamber with a flask of whisky and treated the men to a dram after admiring their work. Replacing the flask in his hip pocket, he climbed out of the chamber, forgetting that his flask was now full of compressed air, so that when he emerged out of the airlock at the top, into normal atmospheric pressure, it exploded.

At Queensferry the sea-bed was different from that at Inchgarvie, and the problem of laying secure foundations correspondingly so. Baker describes the work:

> At Queensferry all four piers were founded on caissons identical in principle with those used for the deep Garvie piers. The deepest was 89 feet below high water, and weighed 20,000 tons; the shallowest of the four was 71 feet high, the diameter in all cases, as at Garvie being 70 feet at the base . . . . Instead of a sloping surface of rock (as at Inchgarvie), the bed of the Forth was of soft mud to a considerable depth, through which the caissons had to be sunk into hard boulder clay. [In fact the caissons had to be sunk twenty-three feet through mud and silt before reaching the necessary firm base.] Double skins were provided for the caissons, between which concrete could be filled in to various heights if necessary, so that greater weight might be applied to the cutting edge where the mud was hard than where it was soft.

On New Year's Day 1884, while one of the Queensferry caissons was being moved into position, an exceptionally high tide, followed by a very low ebb occurred, and the vast cylinder tipped over. Stuck well and truly in the mud it filled with water when the tide rose again, resulting in its sinking still further. In a rush to get rid of the water, the men worked the pumps too quickly, with the result that some of the plating buckled under the pressure of water outside before the carpenters had had time to install internal stiffening timbers. Righting the caisson again took ten months and necessitated surrounding the whole cylinder with a timber "barrel" which reached above the high-water level, and then pumping out the water and refloating the monster.

If one of the finished piers were to be drawn out of the mud and set in a field it would rise 107 feet into the air and would have a diameter longer than the length of a cricket pitch. It took three years to complete their construction and that of the piers for the approach viaducts at either end of the bridge, and as soon as they were complete, work could start on the erection of the superstructure.

THE SUPERSTRUCTURE

How do you secure a tube of steel weighing nearly 3000 tons, with its superstructure, and stretching for 680 feet at an angle of seventy degrees from the vertical, to the concrete pier that is to support it? This was the initial problem confronting the engineers. They overcame it by first fastening a 44-ton steel plate to the top of the pier with 24-foot long bolts and then attaching to that a structure called a "skewback".

A skewback is the assembly from which the five massive tubular steel main struts in each cantilever spring from the pier. Through it all the loads imposed on the superstructure—both the 3000-ton deadweight and a further possible 3000 tons of wind pressure—passed to the bridge supports. The skewbacks were built on shore and so complicated was their construction that on some days it was possible to close only six rivets in a day (building the central towers, up to 800 rivets were closed in a day). Once complete the skewbacks were floated out and hoisted onto the piers with cranes, then the first sections of the struts that it had to connect—the bottom members, the massive vertical columns, the diagonal columns of the central tower and the first strut of the cantilever, each of them twelve feet in diameter—were riveted into their respective places, and thus connected to the top of the pier.

The next stage was to erect the 350-feet high central tower—the bodies of the men in Baker's illustration. This was constructed using a mechanical riveter, invented by Sir William Arrol. Baker said of this stage in the building:

> The riveting appliances designed by Mr Arrol are of a very special and even formidable character, each machine weighing about sixteen tons. It consists essentially of an inside and outside hydraulic ram mounted on longitudinal and annular girders in such a manner as to command every rivet in the tubes and to close the same by hydraulic pressure. Pipes from the hydraulic pumps are carried up inside the tubes to the riveters, and oil furnaces for heating the rivets are placed in convenient spots, also inside the tubes. By practice and with the stimulus of premiums the men have succeeded in putting in 800 rivets a day with one of these machines at a height of three hundred feet above the sea, which in fact is more than they accomplished when working at ground level. Indeed by the system of erection adopted, the element of height is practically annihilated, and with ordinary caution the men are safer aloft than below, as in the former case they are not liable to have things dropped on their heads.

Once the towers were standing the successive bays of the cantilevers could be added to right and left, balancing each side up all the time as work progressed, until the great arms leant over and reached the arm approaching from the neighbouring cantilever.

Work went on day and night and only stopped when bad weather, particularly strong wind, made it foolish to risk men in such exposed positions above the Forth. Lighting the site was a considerable problem. Gas in South Queensferry was exorbitantly expensive (it was still sold by volume, not by thermal units, and cost 8/4d per 1000 cubic feet) and Lucigen oil lamps, though robust and powerful were prone to spillage and thus made the girders slippery and dangerous. The company opted for the new electric lighting, arc lighting for outdoor work and incandescent lamps for indoors. The arc lighting, in spite of being the best available at the time, was still very varied in its illumination: it tended to flicker, and intervening objects—girders or struts—cast very black shadows. Moreover, since the lights were arranged in a circuit driven by a dynamo, a simple defect anywhere along the line would extinguish twenty or thirty lights without warning, at once plunging into darkness men who were often working in very precarious situations, and who did not know whether to struggle on and trust to their own eyesight or to stand stock-still until the lights came on again.

Another difficulty was that the positioning of the lights altered daily as the massive structure changed shape, and this made navigation on the Forth in bad weather hazardous in the extreme. One ship, a tug, rammed the quay at North Queensferry, damaging both the quay and the barge that it was towing, and after this it was decided to built a lighthouse on Inchgarvie, with a light that could be seen for twelve miles up and down the river. This lighthouse is still operating. Even though many difficulties were overcome, however, it was estimated that work after dark was never better than fifty per cent of daytime productivity.

COMPLETION

Because of the variation due to temperature possible in such a phenomenal amount of

The Forth Bridge under construction

The Forth Bridge works, Fife Piers, from Coastguard Hill, August 1886

Opposite: The Forth Bridge from the north side, August 3rd, 1887

steel, it was crucial that the central girders linking the cantilevers and completing the bridge were attached at a mean temperature— on a cloudy day or at night. The idea was to make a temporary connection and then to complete the final fastening in a matter of hours, when the temperature was even. Baker described the final connection:

By 28th October the last booms were put out, and by 6th November everything was ready to connect the girder also. The temperature on that day did not rise, however, sufficiently high to make the joint but in the night a sudden rise took place, and by 7.30 in the morning the bottom booms were joined together for good. It now required a good fall of the temperature to get the top booms connected, for the two halves of this girder had been set less high at starting, and there was now practically no camber in the bottom booms. But the weather remained obstinate and the temperature very high, and it was not until the morning of 14th November that the key plates could be driven in and the final connection made. An episode of which much has been made in the papers occurred on this occasion, and the facts are simply as follows.

After the wedges at the bottom ends had been drawn out and the key plates driven in, a slight rise in temperature was indicated by the thermometer in the course of the morning, and orders were given to remove the bolts in the central joints of the connecting ties and to light the furnaces. Whether the thermometer indicated wrongly or whether a decrease of the same took place, it is not now possible to prove, but when only about 36 of the turned steel bolts remained in the joints and before the furnaces could get fairly started, the plate ties sheared the remaining bolts and parted with a bang like a shot from a 38-ton gun.

Something of a shake occurred in the cantalevers, which was felt at the opposite ends and caused some little commotion among the men. No mishap occurred, however, and nothing in the way of a fall of the girders took place as stated in the papers, simply the work of the furnaces and the task of knocking out thirty-six bolts was saved, and the girder swung on its rockers as freely as if it had been freed in the most natural manner.

The first person to cross the bridge officially had in fact crossed it a month before, on 15th October, 1889: this was M.W. Thompson, the Chairman of the Forth Bridge Railway Company, with his board of directors, and they walked across a temporary gangway that had been erected across the gap. There was still much to do, however, before the bridge was ready for use, and it took a further four months before the Prince of Wales was able to drive home the last rivet and declare the structure open.

THE OPENING CEREMONY

The day of the opening ceremony, 4th March 1890, was wet and windy. *Railway Press*, a journal now long out of print, described the crowds of people and vehicles along the Queensferry Road, and noted that "the usually dull burgh of South Queensferry presented an animated and busy appearance".

A train-load of dignitaries followed by another consisting of the Royal Party crossed the Bridge and ran to Inverkeithing and then to the pier at North Queensferry. There everyone embarked for a sight-seeing trip of inspection of the Bridge from sea-level before returning to their trains at the quayside. The Royal Train left first, and stopped in the middle of the north connecting girder where the Prince performed the last rivet hammering ceremony. The train then stopped again on the south cantilever where the actual opening ceremony was performed. The weather was so boisterous that the Prince just had to curtail his speech to merely announcing that the Bridge was opened. Although it was not raining, toppers kept getting blown off

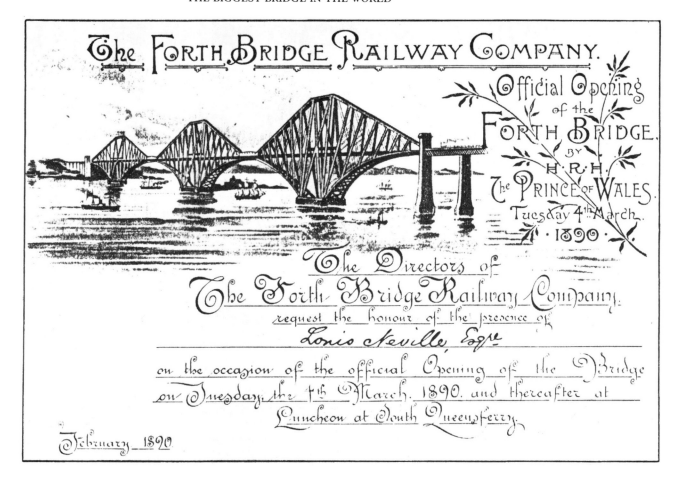

Invitation to the Official Opening of the Forth Bridge, 4 March
1890

Back cover and front cover (opposite) of the luncheon menu for the Opening Ceremony of the Forth Bridge.

OFFICIAL OPENING
of the FORTH BRIDGE
Tuesday 4th March
1890.

THRO CARRIAGE. ABERDEEN TO NEW YORK. VIA TAY BRIDGE,
FORTH BRIDGE, CHANNEL TUNNEL AND ALASKA

N·B·R

PROGRESS

"Of dazzling great adventures
this, the foremost."

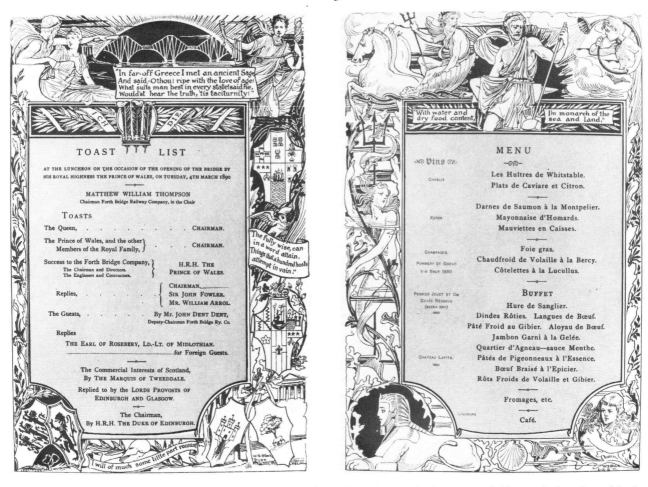

In far-off Greece I met an ancient Sage
And said—Othou! ripe with the love of age!
What suits man best in every state said he,
Would'st hear the truth, 'tis taciturnity!'

The fully wise, can in a word attain,
Things that a hundred hosts attempt in vain.'

TOAST LIST

AT THE LUNCHEON ON THE OCCASION OF THE OPENING OF THE BRIDGE BY
HIS ROYAL HIGHNESS THE PRINCE OF WALES, ON TUESDAY, 4TH MARCH 1890

MATTHEW WILLIAM THOMPSON
Chairman Forth Bridge Railway Company, in the Chair

TOASTS

The Queen,	CHAIRMAN.
The Prince of Wales, and the other Members of the Royal Family,	CHAIRMAN.
Success to the Forth Bridge Company, The Chairman and Directors. The Engineers and Contractors.	H.R.H. THE PRINCE OF WALES.
Replies,	CHAIRMAN. SIR JOHN FOWLER. MR. WILLIAM ARROL.
The Guests,	By MR. JOHN DENT DENT, Deputy-Chairman Forth Bridge Ry. Co.

Replies

THE EARL OF ROSEBERY, LD.-LT. OF MIDLOTHIAN.
.......for Foreign Guests.

The Commercial Interests of Scotland,
By THE MARQUIS OF TWEEDDALE.

Replied to by the LORDS PROVOSTS OF
EDINBURGH AND GLASGOW.

The Chairman,
By H.R.H. THE DUKE OF EDINBURGH.

I will of much some little part recount

'With water and dry food content,'   'I'm monarch of the sea and land.'

MENU

Vins	
CHABLIS	Les Huîtres de Whitstable. Plats de Caviare et Citron.
XERES	Darnes de Saumon à la Montpelier. Mayonnaise d'Homards. Mauviettes en Caisses.
CHAMPAGNE POMMERY ET GRENO VIN BRUT 1880	Foie gras. Chaudfroid de Volaille à la Bercy. Côtelettes à la Lucullus.
PERRIER JOUET ET CIE CUVÉE RÉSERVE (EXTRA DRY) 1880	**BUFFET** Hure de Sanglier. Dindes Rôties. Langues de Bœuf. Pâté Froid au Gibier. Aloyau de Bœuf. Jambon Garni à la Gelée. Quartier d'Agneau—sauce Menthe.
CHATEAU LAFITE 1880	Pâtés de Pigeonneaux à l'Essence. Bœuf Braisé à l'Epicier. Rôts Froids de Volaille et Gibier.
LIQUEURS	Fromages, etc. Café.

The designer of the menu card had obviously been given free rein to indulge in fantasy and allegory in keeping with the period. Above are the inside pages of the menu for the Opening Ceremony luncheon.

THE OPENING OF THE FORTH BRIDGE: *No photographs are known to exist of this historic occasion. The illustration is from "Our Railways" by J. Pendelton, published in 1896, and depicts H.R.H. The Prince of Wales in the* company of Sir William Arrol, Lord Rosebery, Sir Benjamin Baker, The Marquis of Tweeddale, and others. The Prince is driving home the last rivet which was gilded for the occasion.

NORTH BRITISH RAILWAY ENGINE No. 602
This locomotive hauled the inaugural royal train at the opening of
the Bridge and was rewarded with the honour of carrying the
Prince of Wales' Feathers along with the motto 'Ich dien' on her
front driving splashers. The engine had 7-foot coupled wheels and
ran until 1926 when she was withdrawn. She remained as the
N.B.R. royal engine. The first engine of this class, No. 592, was
built in 1886 and was shown at the Edinburgh Exhibition of that
year, having arrived under her own steam on temporary rails laid
on the city streets.

everyone's heads, and the train was moved on a bit because of the steam which was blowing right across the proceedings.

The banquet which followed the ceremony was held in the engineers' model room at the South Queensferry works, which had been lavishly decorated in crimson, rose and gold, with shields bearing the devices of the great railway companies and the arms of towns in England and Scotland, and a great crimson-and-gold plush canopy over the high table. The Prince ended his speech of thanks by saying:

I have much pleasure in stating that, on the recommendation of the Prime Minister, the Queen has been pleased to create Mr. Thompson, Chairman of the Forth Bridge Company, and of the Midland Railway Company, and Sir John Fowler, engineer-in-chief of the Forth Bridge, baronets of the United Kingdom. The Queen has also created, or intends to create, Mr. Benjamin Baker, Sir John Fowler's colleague, a K.C.M.G., and to confer on Mr William Arrol, the contractor, the honour of a knighthood.

4

THE ENGINEERS

The lesson which the Forth Bridge teaches us is that there are no natural obstacles, no rivers, I may add no channels, too wide or too deep for the Engineer. Let only the public or commerce make the demand, and *the work, however gigantic will be executed.*

(The Marquis of Tweeddale at the Opening Banquet; March 4th, 1890.)

Sir John Fowler (1817-1898)

It is difficult in a world familiar with neutron bombs and moon landings, to appreciate the enormity of the task facing the bridge builders. In a century marked by a dynamic growth in heavy engineering, the Forth Rail Bridge was an engineering project of unprecedented proportions—and required engineers and contractors of outstanding ability.

Sir John Fowler, the chief engineer, was born at Wadsley Hall, Sheffield, in 1817. After completing a general education he was apprenticed to J.T. Leather, an eminent hydraulic engineer. This was a period of extraordinary industrial expansion, and there was ample employment for engineers. Fowler quickly gained valuable experience on large works such as the water supply scheme for Sheffield Corporation and benefited substantially from being encouraged to be versatile rather than being channelled along highly specialised lines.

On leaving Mr Leather's service as a fully qualified practical engineer Fowler entered the office of the famous J.U. Rastrick, the railway engineer with a large and varied practice. Soon he became chief assistant drawing up plans and documents for several proposed railways, among which was the line from London to Brighton. After two years Fowler returned to the service of Mr Leather, as resident engineer on the Stockton and Hartlepool Railway. Moving from one responsible post to another, he regarded every new job as a challenge, for most of the problems he was confronted with could not be answered from textbooks. At the early age of twenty-six, having been general manager and locomotive superintendent of the Stockton and Hartlepool and the Clarence Railway, he was asked to visit several proposed sites for railways in and around Glasgow.

The year 1843 marked the beginning of the Railway Mania, when speculators made and lost fortunes in a day; it was a time when enormous capital sums were invested in railways of every type, and when normally shrewd businessmen often squandered their entire capital, and that of other people, on schemes supported only by rumour and hearsay. Fowler was by now launched on an independent career as a consulting engineer, giving evidence before Parliamentary Committees, and being involved in many of the important railways being promoted from Sheffield, notably the Sheffield and Lincolnshire, the Great

Grimsby (around which there was such speculation that Lord Devon, chairman of the Parliamentary Committee, exclaimed "What! Great Grimsby again? Go it, Great Grimsby!"), the New Holland and the East Lincolnshire Railways.

Despite finding himself in the thick of the Railway Mania, Fowler managed to maintain his careful and balanced judgement. There were occasions, however, when that judgement was sorely tested. For example, one night in 1844 he was woken in the middle of the night by a well-known railway promoter. The promoter tried to induce him to undertake all the engineering work for a new railway from Leeds to Glasgow. As a guarantee of good faith, he brought with him a cheque for £20,000 to defray surveying expenses. Fowler who was by now no stranger to being offered madcap schemes, wisely declined the offer.

Those extraordinary times claimed many victims from the ranks of hitherto competent and respectable engineers, many of whom might have risen to the top of their profession had they not wantonly sacrificed their time and efforts on promoting unsound and wasteful schemes. Only engineers of the highest professional integrity, thoroughly sound in both mind and body, managed to come through unscathed. The Engineer's job was by no means completed on the deposit of plans, because the Engineer responsible for drawing up a set of plans for a proposed railway was required to attend Parliamentary Committees, for which a great deal of preparation was necessary, in order to defend the proposed plans against the opposing counsels who were backed by engineers of their own. The Committee proceedings were followed with the keenest interest by many who had no understanding of engineering principles but who knew that the outcome of the meeting might be used to manipulate the stockmarket to advantage.

Gambling in Railway Stock was on a fantastic scale, with investors being influenced in their choice of investment by the merest trifles: so much so that on one occasion Fowler said that he met an aquaintance rushing down a corridor in the House of Commons, who, when Fowler stopped him, brushed brusquely past shouting, "Don't detain me! Robert Stephenson has broken down in his attack, and I'm off to buy a thousand Great Northerns." John Francis in his *A History of the English Railway* (London 1851) noted that "the traffic of the country had trebled within the previous twenty one years" and that "in 1843 seventy rail-roads had conveyed 25,000,000 passengers for 330,000,000 miles with only three fatal accidents . . . . at an average cost of 1¾d each person." By 1845, 2,000 miles of railway had been completed by forty-seven companies, at a cost of £70,500,000. In addition to the completed tracks there were 1,263 proposals for new railways in respect of which £59,000,000 had to be deposited before they could be considered by Parliament.

Although the railway boom continued through the spring and summer of 1843, many of those intimately involved with the Railway Mania began to suspect that the air of insupportable fantasy had begun to surround railway developments. The Chairman of the Great Western Railway issued a warning against the multiplicity of lines, and when the Bank of England raised the bank rate in October 1845, confidence evaporated, panic began to set in, and share prices began to slip, reaching their lowest level in 1848. In April 1849, the empire of Hudson, the "Railway King", collapsed. He resigned from Chairmanship of the Midland Railway. Fowler benefited considerably from this as the importance of the Manchester, Sheffield and Lincolnshire was increased.

In those uncertain times Fowler won himself a reputation for reliability, a quality which he regarded as being the guiding principle of the professional engineer. "It is not the business," (T.Mackay records Fowler as saying in his *Life of Sir John Fowler*) "of an engineer to build a fine bridge or to construct a magnificent engineering work for the purpose of displaying his professional attainments, but, whatever the temptation may be, his duty is to accomplish this end and aim of his employers by such works and such means as are, on the whole, the best and most economically adapted for the purpose."

Fowler's continued success was not based entirely on his reputation for reliability. He had an abundance of commonsense and a sledgehammer directness in his dealings at all levels. The evidence he was called upon to submit to Parliamentary Committees was always clear, concise and strictly to the point. He never hesitated to speak his mind, and when his close friend and arguably the greatest engineer of his age, I.K. Brunel, died in 1859, and Fowler was appointed consulting civil engineer to the Great Western Railway, he did not delay in recommending to the directors that they abandon the broad gauge, which was a peculiarity of the Great Western Railway lines and which had been particularly favoured by Brunel. T. Mackay succinctly summarised Fowler's character when he wrote that "as an engineer he had of course many equals from a scientific point of view, but he was so eminently practical that nothing beat him, and his power of dealing with men was wonderful."

Above all, Fowler was in tune with the spirit of the age. Rapid and intensive industrial development required that new ideas, methods and materials be used to their utmost effect. While not being the instigator of any great advances in civil engineering he was one of the first in his profession to realise that timber would have to be replaced by iron and steel, and that steel railway tracks were infinitely more durable than iron ones. He was also one of the first to advocate the use of Portland cement in the construction of retaining walls. Like all great generals Fowler was good at delegating responsibility. Extremely hard-working and diligent himself,

he inspired these qualities in his subordinates, in whom he placed complete trust.

Although by 1860 Fowler had been made responsible for many projects, some of which were to influence him in his plans for the Forth Bridge (the Wicker viaduct, Sheffield Victoria Station, New Holland floating bridge and especially the two cast iron bridges spanning the Severn), his public reputation rested on the construction of the Metropolitan Railway. Despite universal forebodings of failure, and engineering difficulties that most believed were insurmountable, together with numerous problems with local authorities and property owners and their agents, Fowler completed the project with such success that even experienced specialists were incredulous. The first section of the Metropolitan Railway was opened on January 9th, 1863; and in April of that year Fowler submitted a statement to Gladstone, which recorded that 2,000,000 passengers had been carried in the three months since opening, and that 60,000 had been carried on one day. To Fowler's eternal disappointment his proposed plans for an Outer Circle were never taken up; and although he carried out further projects such as the St John's Wood Railway, the West Brompton line and the Hammersmith line, he was never reconciled to Parliament's piecemeal approach, as he saw from the outset the enormous benefits which a comprehensive scheme would have brought.

It was rare for Fowler to be thwarted in his plans, for although he formed his opinion with instinctive quickness, and held on to it firmly, never questioning its soundness himself, he almost never failed to satisfy most of his hearers with his persuasive reasoning.

In 1885 Fowler was knighted for his services to the Khedive of Egypt, and stood as Conservative candidate for Hallamshire, in his home county of Yorkshire. He soon discovered that canvassing was an exhausting business, and as the Forth Bridge was demanding most of his time already, he retired from the contest on medical advice. This step was applauded by the directors of the Forth Bridge, and one of them, Mr Dent, wrote to Sir John saying, "I am very glad that you have given up Hallamshire: the successful finish of the Forth Bridge is a greater crown to a man's life than a seat in Parliament."

The Forth Bridge was indeed the crown to Sir John's professional career, and confident in the knowledge that his business affairs were more than ably administered by his partner Sir Benjamin Baker, he busied himself in his latter years with improving his vast Highland estate "Braemore".

Sir Benjamin Baker (1840-1907)

Benjamin Baker was born in Glamorganshire, on March 31st 1840. Having been educated at home, when he was sixteen he was apprenticed to Messrs Price and Fox, at the Neath Abbey Iron Works. At Neath Abbey he gained a thoroughly practical knowledge of the basic principles of engineering practice, and throughout his later career he had little time for engineering theory unsupported by practical experience. After serving a hard but valuable apprenticeship he was engaged as an assistant to Mr W.H. Wilson in the construction of Victoria Station. This was ideal experience for the young Baker, as the project was fraught with engineering problems.

From 1862 onwards he worked under John Fowler on the construction of the Metropolitan and St John's Wood lines. He used what spare time he had to study theoretical mechanics; and published the results of his studies in a series of articles entitled "Long Span Bridges" in *Engineering*, which was then the profession's most respected journal. The articles were so favourably received by engineers all over the world, that they were re-published in book form in England, the United States, Germany and Austria. They revealed that traditional and highly unsatis-factory approximate methods were being superceded by a scientific approach to structural problems. Baker had a remarkable faculty to see the root of the problem and identify the principal elements, without being led astray by insignificancies and needless complexities, which were a waste of both time and money. In the articles he devoted careful study to the merits of the cantilever principle and hence helped to prepare himself for the problems he would encounter when designing the Forth Bridge.

Having completed the Herculean task of constructing the District line from Westminster to the City, Baker was then sent by Fowler to Egypt to draw up plans for the Khedive for a combined irrigation and ship canal linking Cairo and Alexandria. This was intended to be much larger than the Suez Canal, but because several large ships had been commissioned especially for the Suez Canal, the project was abandoned. Instead, in 1878, Baker's skills were called upon to help transport Cleopatra's Needle from Egypt to England. After several mishaps the obelisk was brought to the Thames, but there the contractor, John Dixon, was at a loss as to how to erect the Needle onto its pedestal without damaging the ancient carvings. Under Baker's instructions a large timber structure was built and the Needle raised in a horizontal position, pivotted at its centre of gravity. It was then turned on a knife edge framework into a vertical position and lowered onto the pedestal. The plan worked perfectly, and its devisor received considerable public acclaim for his ingenuity. When his design for the Forth Bridge was accepted Baker's reputation was firmly established, and he was given the opportunity to put into practice in one structure all the conclusions that he had reached since 1867.

From the commencement of building in 1883 until completion in 1890, Baker virtually lived on site, where, alongside his considerable supervisory duties, he conducted a series of experiments in the properties of structural steel. Always preferring simple and logical construction, Baker was of the firm opinion that the underlying question behind any engineering project was the fitness for purpose of any structural materials used. Thus his primary concern with the Bridge was that it should be efficient and simple as a structure, and that if these rules of simplicity and efficiency were adhered to the Bridge would "work". Secondary concerns often required ingenious and sophisticated engineering, and on the Forth Bridge Baker showed himself to be as equal to these challenges as he was to that of the overall structure. For example, he designed an internal track to carry the railway line that ran across the Bridge, so that if a train was derailed while on the Bridge the wheels would drop into troughs and would be able to continue to the end of the Bridge.

After completing the Forth Railway Bridge, and being knighted for his services to engineering, Sir Benjamin Baker went on to other great achievements, most notable of which was the old Aswan Dam in Egypt. Like his partner, Sir John Fowler, he became President of the Institute of Civil Engineers as well as laying the foundations of what is now the British Standards Institution. For his services on the Aswan Dam he was awarded the K.C.B. and was also invested with the Order of Medjidie, First Class. He was elected a Fellow of the Royal Society in addition to being awarded the Poncelet Prize of the French Academy of Sciences. There is a memorial window to him in Westminster Abbey.

Sir William Arrol (1839-1913)

In stark contrast to the privileged upbringing and education of the chief engineers, Sir William Arrol, the contractor for the Bridge, rose to eminence from the humblest origins. Born February 13th 1839, in Renfrewshire, he was the son of a cotton spinner and the fourth son in a family of nine children. His father, Thomas Arrol, was seriously injured when William was still in his infancy, and the awesome task of bringing up the young family fell on his mother.

When only nine William went to work as a 'piercer' at a cotton mill in Johnstone, and when his family moved to Paisley in 1850 he found employment in Coats' Thread Manufactory. At the age of fourteen he apprenticed himself to a blacksmith in Paisley, while attending night-school in the shop of a weaver who taught mathematics. Having served his time, and determined to improve himself, he found a job as a journeyman blacksmith in a Clyde shipyard. Here he not only gained valuable experience, but set up his own business mending porridge pots and kitchen utensils.

Times were hard and in the seven years after completing his apprenticeship he found it difficult to get regular employment. He travelled from town to town and at last found regular work at Kerr's factory in Paisley, where, although he earned only 22/- a week, the job was very varied and helped to broaden his experience. There followed a brief spell in the army, after which he was engaged as foreman at Laidlaw's Engineering Works in Glasgow, where he earned £2 per week.

In 1868 Arrol set up in business on his own, with a capital backing of only £250, and despite a few initial set-backs, was able to enlarge his works and to accept a contract to construct a series of bridges over the Water of Leith between Edinburgh and Balerno. In 1872 he built his famous works at Dalmarnock, and in 1875 undertook the construction of the North British Railway bridge over the Clyde at Bothwell. This project brought him before the public eye for the first time, and he amply demonstrated his ingenuity by devising a scheme for constructing cantilever girders on land and rolling them out from pier to pier over the water, rather than assembling them over the river. This saved time and money, as well as minimising the risk to the workforce.

Later in 1875 he undertook the construction of the first of his two famous Caledonian bridges, over the Clyde at Broomielaw. During the erection of this bridge he invented a hydraulic riveting machine that could clench seven rivets in a minute. This invention meant that the riveting on the bridge was not only more efficient but was done for half the cost of hand riveting. This machine was to play an important part in the construction of the Forth Bridge.

W.H. Barlow was commissioned to design the replacement Tay Bridge and he instructed Arrol as the contractor. Work started on the new Tay Bridge in 1882 and finished in 1887, so for five years Arrol was supervising both projects. The work that this involved was immense, and was commented on at the opening ceremony for the Forth Bridge, when the Prince of Wales said in his speech that both Forth and Tay Bridges "will be a lasting monument of his (Arrol's) skill, resources and energy".

During the time that the bridges were being constructed Arrol would wake at five in the morning in order to be at his Glasgow works by six. Once at the works, he carefully reviewed the previous day's progress on both structures and explained to his senior staff the plans and procedures that were necessary. After a light breakfast he would then catch the 8.45 train to Edinburgh to begin work at the Bridge. Once at the site he would hold a progress meeting with his department heads and then inspect such parts of the structure as were in progress on that day, visiting the site foremen and encouraging the men. This took most of the day, and then at six o'clock he would board the train for Dundee to inspect the Tay Bridge site. Sometimes his consultations went on well into the night, but he would always catch the train back to Glasgow in order to be in his Dalmarnock works at six

the next morning. The only variation in his schedule was that on Wednesday and Friday he would visit the Tay first, travelling to Queensferry in the evening. On Friday night he took the sleeper to London in order to attend meetings with the consulting engineers of both bridges, returning north on Saturday night.

Arrol kept up his superhuman workload for the full time that it took to complete the Bridge, and he once claimed, when questioned about his health, that the more work he took on the better he felt. He was said to draw inspiration from problems that caused others to despair. Apart from his hydraulic riveter, he was one of the pioneers of prefabrication and the inventor of a mechanical drilling tool. The Forth and Tay Bridges brought him world-wide acclaim as well as a knighthood, and his firm went on to build bridges all over the world, including Tower Bridge in London, in 1894. By the end of the century the firm that he had founded with a capital of £250 was the largest structural engineering company in the country, occupying some twenty acres and employing over 5,000 men. Little did its founder realise that it would be one of the partners in the construction of the Forth Road Bridge, which was completed in 1964.

A progressive thinker, he was concerned with many of the problems of his day. In an article printed in *The Scotsman* of Thursday, February 27th, 1890, a few days prior to the opening of the Forth Bridge, it was reported that Arrol was to receive the honour of the Freedom of the City of Ayr—an honour rarely granted, and previously bestowed upon Kossuth, the Hungarian patriot, and General Ulysses S. Grant. Arrol was quoted as saying:

My character is representative of the working classes of Scotland, as one of those who has been able to raise themselves by their own energy and industry. . . . We do a great deal so that the best of our young men may get a good education and be raised to a higher and better position socially. I am sorry to say that our trades are not benefitting by that, because more people seem to think that their sons are getting a better education than their fathers, and therefore they must be gentlemen and not tradesmen, so that our better young men have learned to be clerks and to follow other light employment. The result is that within the inside of a few years the country is getting overstocked with that class, and I believe thousands and thousands of them would be glad to get half the wages paid to working men. I hold it altogether wrong that so many young men are not learning trades. Give them, certainly, the best education that you can, but at the same time give them a trade along with their education. Our trade has got into the hands of a few, and you cannot get so many decent steady tradesmen. If you advertise for a tradesman you will perhaps get a single application. Whereas if you advertise for a clerk you will get 400 or 500.

Clearly, Sir William Arrol had anticipated a malaise that has dogged British industry right up to the present day.

Of the many fine qualities that Arrol possessed, perhaps the most notable was his loyalty to his political party (he was Liberal Unionist M.P. for South Ayrshire for fourteen years). A notable example of this loyalty came in 1905. His first wife Elizabeth Pattison, who had been mentally disturbed for some years, died in 1903, and Arrol decided to marry his cousin Jessie Hodgart. On his wedding day he was informed of a crucial division in the House of Commons, and without waiting for the reception, he and his new bride left for London immediately after the service, arriving late at night, but just in time for the division. The Marquis of Hamilton was so impressed by Arrol's loyalty on this occasion that he proposed to the party that Arrol be honoured in some way. He was presented with a silver cup "for conspicuous loyalty" by the Prime Minister, A.J. Balfour. It was reported in *The Times* that "no doubt most of them [i.e. the other members] tried to immitate their honourable friend's devotion to the party, but it was given to few of them to afford such a striking example of that virtue". What his new wife thought at the time is not recorded!

Always a modest man, Arrol shunned publicity wherever possible and when presented with the Freedom of the City of Dundee said, "I would rather build two bridges than make one speech."

5

THE BRIGGERS

Many of them—hundreds of them—were mere birds of passage, who arrived on the tramp, worked for a week or two, and passed on again to other parts, bringing a pair of hands with them and taking them away again, and having in the meantime made extremely little use of them except for the purpose of lifting the Saturday pay packet and wiping their mouths at the pot-house. . . . But apart from these, it is no exaggeration to say that no one need desire to have to do with a more civil lot of men. Always ready to oblige, always ready to go where they were told to go, cheerfully obeying orders . . . and above all things, ready to help others in misfortune, not with advice but with hands and purses.
(W. Westhofen, in *Engineering: Forth Bridge Supplement*, February, 1890)

The men who worked on the construction of the Bridge quickly became known as "the Briggers", and, not unlike today's North Sea rig-workers, they earned themselves a reputation for being courageous, hard-working, and hard-playing, men. Sir William Arrol, always very concerned for the welfare of his workforce, once said that "the further a public house is from a public work the better". But while it is true that the crime rate rose in the neighbouring towns when the briggers were about, and that wild weekends led to Monday morning queues outside the Magistrate's Court, this was only to be expected with such an influx of unattached men into the local community.

The briggers were instantly recognisable as they swaggered through the streets of Edinburgh or Leith or Dunfermline or any of the townships within reach of the ferry. Many of them wore bell-bottomed trousers and red spotted scarves, while others wore large iron rings fashioned from scraps of steel found on the Bridge. Most of the briggers were honest, law-abiding citizens and some of them brought their families with them when they came to South Queensferry in search of employment. The men were housed all over the district, either in the special houses built for them at South and North Queensferry, or in lodgings in Dalmeny, Kirkliston, Inverkeithing or Dunfermline. Many briggers decided to stay on after the Bridge had been completed, and their descendants live "in the shadow of the Bridge" to this day.

But not all of the workforce could live in the Bridge's shadow—there was simply not enough room for the 4,000-odd men employed —so special trains were laid on every day from Edinburgh and Leith. A paddle steamer was provided to carry the men across the Forth at Queensferry, making hourly trips carrying workers, materials and visitors. It quickly became known to every tramp and traveller in the country that a free passage was to be had across the Forth, with the possibility of work on the other side, and the service was "much abused". Indeed the number of tramps using it rose at such an alarming rate that

ABOVE: GLENCRAIG IN LARK JEAN MUIR SUIT

RIBBED TIGHTS IN KESTREL

Above: A glamorous example of the use of the Forth Railway Bridge in advertising. This one was used in Vogue magazine to promote the products of Elbeo. The photographer was Graham Hughes.

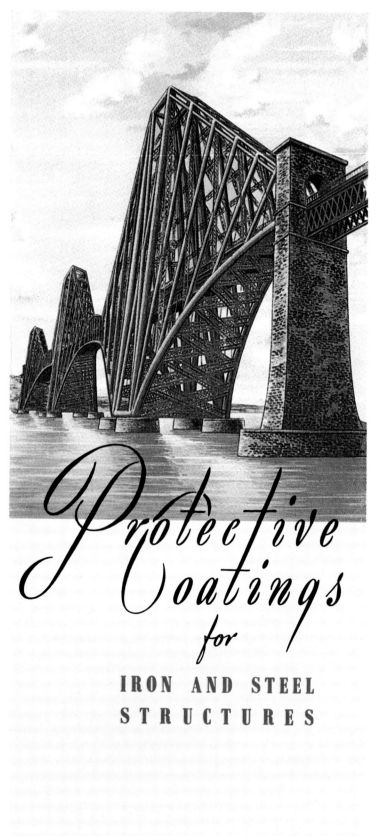

Right: A circular still distributed and provided by courtesy of Messrs. Craig and Rose, who as suppliers of paint for the Bridge, used the famous structure for their trademark.

Below: A Capital Oatcakes tin proudly features both bridges over the Forth. Reproduced here by courtesy of Crawfords.

Protective Coatings

for

IRON AND STEEL
STRUCTURES

Bouch's Forth Bridge got as far as one brick pier which was built on Inch Garvie and now has a lighthouse atop. Work ceased when his Tay Bridge collapsed.

*Before the Forth Bridge: A view of Queensferry drawn by
Clarkson Stanfield, R.A. (1793-1867). The artist was a land-
scape and marine painter who was good enough to earn the
soubriquet of the English Vanderveldt although of Irish descent,
his father being James who was an actor and an author of works
which dealt with anti-slavery.*

*Clarkson was in the navy for six years after 1812 by courtesy
of the press gang, but after demobilisation he painted scenery for
Drury Lane, and on one occasion did a backdrop for Charles
Dickens.*

The Forth Bridge

FORTH BRIDGE EDINBURGH

Forth Bridge

VALENTINES SERIES

Above: An artist's impression of a night scene, published by Valentine and posted from Glasgow, 1903.

Previous page top: A Raphael Tuck & Sons "Art" postcard posted in 1903 from Edinburgh to "Gleska". A cryptic greeting in handwriting on the reverse says: "I really do hope you will enjoy your holiday as it is the last one you will get."

Previous page centre: A product of the Art Publishing Company, Glasgow, posted from North Berwick to Bournemouth in 1907 features the traditional lucky sprig of heather.

Previous page bottom: A Valentine's postcard posted from Edinburgh in 1904 features a winter fantasy by the artist.

Opposite, top: An unused Valentine's postcard shows signs, not entirely uncommon in the early twentieth century, of colour misprinting. The Coastguard Station site suggests remnants of the erstwhile bridge construction.

Opposite, bottom: An unused specimen of B. & R's "Camera" series in which a choice of Scottish names and tartans was available, this one displaying the Cameron. The old Edinburgh coat of arms embellishes the scene.

Overleaf right: A modern view by Victor Albrow.

Forth Bridge and Coastguard Station, North Queensferry

NISI DOMINUS FRUSTRA

EDINBURGH.

CAMERON

THE FORTH BRIDGE.

steps had to be taken to stop the nuisance.

Many of the men came from the Clyde shipyards and the engineering works in the central belt of Scotland and were accustomed to fashioning, riveting and erecting steel plates of a far more complicated shape than those used on the Bridge. They worked at a temendous rate. The sinking of the caissons was in the charge of Monsieur L. Coiseau, a French engineer with wide experience of this sort of work, and he used mainly foreign workmen—North Italians, French, Belgians, Austrians and Germans—with experience of working in the high pressures of the caissons.

Although there were no deaths that could be directly attributed to working in these conditions, Westhofen, who was in charge of Inchgarvie, where the foreign workforce was accommodated and where much of the caisson work was one, remarks that many of those who worked under pressure suffered pains in their joints and muscles. "It has been suggested as a probable cause that small globules of air make their way through the skin, or between the skins, where they remain, and on the workmen returning to ordinary, atmospheric pressure expand, and thereby cause the most agonising pains in the joints, the elbows, shoulders, kneecaps and other places." He remarks that sufferers obtained instant relief upon returning into the high pressure: "Thus it happened that many of those afflicted with this disorder spent the greater part of Saturday afternoon and Sunday under air pressure, and only came out when absolutely obliged to do so." Research was done by medical staff on the site, and continued after the Bridge had been completed. The fruit of it was the discovery of a disease which affects the bones of people working under high pressure, and which in time causes bone death. The disease was named, appropriately, Caissons Disease. Today it is very common amongst divers working in the North Sea.

The rates of pay varied from 4½d an hour for a common labourer to 7d or 8d an hour for riveters. Wages on the whole, however, tended to be above average because there was a great deal of piece-work. As was the custom in engineering or railway work, the men were not directly employed by the company, but by the foreman or ganger of the team that they worked with. Hand riveters, for example, usually worked as a quartet, with two doing the actual riveting, one holding the plate in place and one heating the rivets. The rivet heater was usually a youth, but on him depended the efficiency and earning capacity of the whole squad. Fully aware of their indispensibility, the rivet heating boys usually managed to hold out for a fixed sum of twenty-four shillings a week, regardless of whether the squad worked a full week or not. A squad could, of course, be rendered idle with the absence of one of its members, but, since the pay of the whole squad, distributed by the squad's head riveter, depended on how many rivets were turned and fitted in a week, the company did not lose out. The squad was paid so much for every hundred rivets, with bonus systems operating for particularly hard work.

Drunkenness was a considerable problem during the building of the Bridge; Sir William Arrol himself once commented that he never visited the site without seeing drunken briggers hanging about outside the works. If men were found to be drunk at work they were sent off the site until they sobered up. At one period the drinking became so bad that Arrol instructed that more foreigners be employed, on the principle that they did not drink as much as the Scots! It is probably true to say that it was drink that was responsible for the comparatively high number of accidents in the building of the Bridge: there were many more fatalities during the building of the Forth Bridge than the Tay Bridge, and it has been suggested that this is due to there being no public house within easy reach of the latter.

65

THE OLD WAVERLEY STATION, FROM PRINCES STREET GARDEN
EDINBURGH

Early photograph of the original Waverley Bridge

The Old Town from Princes Street around 1873. The Waverley Bridge—rebuilt in 1873—joins Princes Street with Market Street and Cockburn Street as well as giving access to the station. The Waverley Bridge was rebuilt again, 1890-1900.

The workforce were fortunate in their employers, however; men whose attitude to their employees might have been summed up by Sir Benjamin Baker when he said, "We never ask a workman to do a thing which we are not prepared to do ourselves." In addition to providing temporary housing, Arrol built a reading room and dining room for the men, and at the commencement of building in 1883 he set up a Sick and Accident Club, and, fully aware of the dangers to which the men would be exposed in the construction of the Bridge, made membership compulsory. The way it operated was that every worker had to contribute one hour's pay a week to the fund, with the maximum contribution being limited to 8d. The contractors themselves contributed a further £200 annually, and arranged for free medical advice and medicine for all the members and their families. In addition, the club supported special doctors at Dunfermline, North Queensferry, Edinburgh, Leith, Kirkliston and South Queensferry, provided temporary hospitals at three of the above places and ran an ambulance wagon. If a man was unable to work through sickness or injury he was entitled to between 9/- and 12/- per week in sickness benefit from the Club. The Club also helped to defray members' funeral expenses and made lump-sum payments to the families of men killed or permanently disabled while working on the site.

Despite rigorous safety regulations—hand-rails wherever possible on the superstructure, wire netting being stretched on frames below any exposed point, and lifeboats constantly patrolling the water below—the Bridge claimed fifty-seven lives during the seven years of its construction, or roughly one life every six weeks. Some of the deaths were caused by the reckless disregard for their own safety of many of the younger briggers, who would, for example, jump from girder to girder while working several hundred feet above the ground. Other accidents were

caused by carelessness, and others by drunkenness: Arrol referred to the bar at South Queensferry as the "curse of the works". But the principle reason for the high number of fatalities was simply the extremely dangerous nature of the work. On one occasion, a brigger working at a great height and supporting himself only by hanging onto a rope, became so cold that his hands lost their grip and he fell backwards some 120 feet into the Forth, to be rescued by the watermen in the lifeboat.

Many of the accidents were due to objects falling on men from above: one unfortunate, who was noted for his strength and agility, and who could run hand over hand along a rope at any height, was knocked over by a wedge that had been dropped by a brigger higher up and fell to his death. Sir Benjamin Baker reported that he had seen a spanner pass through a four-inch thick timber staging after it had fallen about 300 feet, and on another occasion he saw a tool drop from a great height into a workman's pocket and come out at his ankle, tearing his clothes off in the process, but leaving him completely unharmed.

The dangers that the men were exposed to increased as the work progressed, but even in the early stages there were accidents. The capsizing of one of the South Queensferry caissons during which two men were drowned has already been referred to, and there is a sinister story about two men being trapped at the bottom of a pier after work had been completed higher up, closing their exit. It proved impossible to undo the work that had been done above, and, after the ganger in charge of the operation had made arrange-ments with the next of kin, poisoned food was sent down to the men prior to the pier being completely sealed off. (It should be stated that this story is hearsay only and doesn't appear in any of the written accounts of the building of the Bridge.)

The worst accident occurred on June 2nd,

1887, when an insecurely fastened staging collapsed, taking six men with it. They were working at a considerable height, and two of the men struck a girder during their fall and were killed before they reached the water below; two others fell clear of the girders and were rescued from the Forth uninjured; and the remaining two caught hold of struts high above the water. Their rescue was no easy matter but after a time the rescuers reached the first man. He gallantly told his saviours to carry on to the other man, as he was more likely to lose his grip. Fortunately both were saved, thanks mainly to the unselfish behaviour of the first man. Although this accident had been brought about entirely by the carelessness of the men involved and not by any fault of the contractors, the event precipitated one of the few strikes to take place during the building of the Bridge. The demand was for a penny an hour more (the equivalent of a 20% pay rise) because of the dangerous nature of the work. Little came of the strike however, as it was soon discovered that the most vociferous speakers at strike meetings were workers in the assembly yards, far removed from the dangerous high girders. The strikers held out for a week and it is recorded that most were glad to get back to work after that period.

Despite the contractors' concern about the welfare of the workforce—the supply of good facilities and shelter, boots and proper working clothes, and so on, and their sparing no expense in constructing secure stagings, gangways and companionways—three-quarters of all the serious accidents that occurred were due to preventible causes. The briggers' familiarity with danger bred contempt for it, and in most cases they worked on stagings cluttered with tools, seemingly oblivious to the risks. Time and again they were warned, and still they ignored the most elementary safety rules. It needed a bad accident to bring home to them the seriousness of the situation.

As careful as the contractors were, the Board of Trade inspectors were not satisfied that enough was being done to prevent accidents. They reported in 1887: "We regret to have to notice that the percentage of fatal accidents to the men employed upon the works had increased, no less than seven men having lost their lives in the last quarter." They went on to say, "We ourselves noticed when on top of the North Queensferry pier, an accident due entirely to the carelessness or ignorance of a foreman; this providentially had no ill results, but might easily have caused loss of life."

Much correspondence appeared in the press about the number of accidents and the precautions that should be taken, and in September 1887 the contractors were forced to send a letter to the newspapers, to counter "the exaggerated reports" on the number of accidents on the Bridge. The letter stated that, "all that good appliances, safeguards and supervision can do we try our best to maintain, but we cannot contend against recklessness or thoughtlessness of the men themselves". This did not, however, quell the mounting public protest, and when two deaths occurred shortly after the publication of the contractors' letter, Andrew Cunningham, editor of the *Dunfermline Journal,* wrote in his editorial that "the monthly slaughter cannot be tolerated; the warnings of the government inspectors seem to be blown over the cantilevers like morning mist". Cunningham wanted special safety inspectors to be appointed. Such a suggestion was strongly opposed by the engineers and the contractors who felt that it would interfere unduly with the management of the works. In the end the government inspectors reluctantly had to admit that "It is very difficult to persuade many of the men to adopt the most ordinary precautions."

In spite of this criticism of the foolhardiness of the men, when the inspectors made their final report there was a special tribute to all who had been involved in the project:

In conclusion we think it right to record our opinion that this great undertaking, every part of which we have seen at different stages of its construction, is a wonderful example of thoroughly good workmanship with excellent materials and that both in its conception and in its execution it is a credit to all who have been connected with it, bearing testimony to the ability of the engineers who have designed it, to the skill and resource of those who have superintended and constructed it, and to the zeal and courage of the workmen who have been employed upon it.

Old buildings at the Scotland Street Station, Edinburgh

6

THE 1890s AND THE FORTH BRIDGE

The Forth Bridge Railway Company

The Forth Bridge Railway Company managed to maintain a separate existence right up until nationalisation after the Second World War. The four original railway companies which comprised it each provided their chairman and vice-chairman and two further directors were elected by the general body of shareholders. The chairmanship of the company was held in rotation by the four railway chairmen for a term of office of twelve months.

The first Board of the company consisted of M.W. Thompson, chairman, and M.U. Heygate of the Midland Railway; Lord Colville and Lord Hindlip of the Great Northern Railway; John Dent-Dent, deputy chairman, and Sir Matthew Ridley, Bt., of the North-Eastern Railway; and the Earl of Elgin and Kincardine of the North British Railway. The shareholders elected Spencer Brunton and James Hall Renton.

Many of the engineers and contractors of the Bridge were kept on. Indeed some others were hired to help with the new approach lines. The Secretary of the North British Railway, G.B. Wieland, was engaged as Secretary. For maintenance of the Bridge, about fifty men comprised a permanent staff, of which some thirty painters were the most

numerous. Others included a couple of watchmen, a joiner, a fitter, a blacksmith, a lighthousekeeper, boatmen and a plumber.

With about 145 acres of steelwork to cover, adequate paint for the bridge weighed some fifty tons and took three years to apply, by which time the first lot was due for renewal. So it has continued. As with the other materials which went into the making of the Bridge, the suppliers kept rigidly to the specifications with some pride. "Forth Bridge Paint" stencilled on the firm's drums was the hallmark of quality. An early specification read:

Pure oxide of iron paint ground in genuine linseed oil guaranteed over 90 per cent in the dry of oxide of iron F_2O_3 of natural origin . . . 9 tons
Red lead . . . 3 tons 12 cwt.
Boiled linseed oil . . . 1,000 gallons
Terebine . . . 50 gallons
Turpentine . . . 50 gallons
Tar Oil . . . 20 gallons
Bituminous viaduct solution . . . 200 gallons

All operations on the Bridge were controlled from the engineer's office perched high up on the structure. A wind gauge was installed as a safety measure and was under constant observation. As soon as a wind of thirty miles per hour or over was recorded, the workmen were ordered off the more exposed parts of the structure. The engineer-in-chief fixed a train speed limit of forty miles per hour. Although this was constantly being broken and drivers were constantly being reported to the North British Railway, little was ever done about it until one driver crossed the Bridge in one-and-a-half minutes flat—equivalent to sixty miles per hour! He was suspended for three days.

Employees of the Forth Bridge as a rule felt themselves to be a breed apart and it was not until 1906 that the North British Railway Company recognised them as railwaymen proper, thus entitling them to an issue of privilege tickets—a "perquisite" as important to a railwayman as the issue of free coal to a miner. It is interesting to note that until comparatively modern times the men of the Forth Bridge Railway Company continued to wear a badge with the insignia "F.B.R.".

At any rate, until it became vested in the British Transport Commission Act of 1947, the company always paid its way as a separate concern. Its revenue was derived from tolls paid by the operating company—the North British Railway, later the London & North Eastern Railway. For rating purposes the Bridge was reckoned to be nineteen miles long. Even during the reduced business period of the North British Railway strike of 1891 the Company managed a healthy profit. For the half-year ending 1892, the traffic receipts amounted to £53,000 to which sum was added a modest £200 for rents and odds and ends. Expenses for that period were £2,000 for maintenance, £875 for general charges, £95 for legal expenses, £315 for compensation, and just under £3,000 for rates and taxes. The result was a profit of about £47,000 for distribution of dividends. On a more solemn note, it must also be stated that the company accounts frequently showed compensation paid as a result of accidents to employees. In 1891, for instance, the sum of £55.5.0 was paid to the widow and eight children of James Smith, who had fallen off the South Approach Viaduct.

The Approach Railways

The railway map of the East of Scotland north of the Forth changed considerably after the opening of the Forth Rail Bridge. It was not just a question of continuing the line from Inverkeithing to Burntisland in order to avoid the Granton ferry: many lines had to be widened and doubled, and a new loop line from Kelty to Cowdenbeath had to be built.

A railway from Mawcarse, through Glenfarg, provided a new route to Perth, which gave the North British access to both the north-east and the north-west of the country. Furthermore the new line meant that the North British was no longer dependent on running powers over its rival, the Caledonian.

Instead of having to go via Larbert, Dundee and Aberdeen could now be reached by Inverkeithing, Burntisland and the Tay Bridge; whilst the Highland Railway's territory to the north of Perth could be reached via Inverkeithing, Glenfarg and Bridge of Earn. The connection from Winchburgh to the south approach lines of the Bridge opened a direct route from Glasgow and the west which avoided Edinburgh altogether. Most of these lines have now been closed and it is no longer possible to travel from Glasgow to Fife without changing at Edinburgh, Haymarket.

The connecting railways entailed heavy

MAWCARSE. Junction of the Glenfarg and the Perth to Dundee lines, the latter going to the right.

An interesting period photograph depicting handwork in iron, steel, masonry, and timber. The two signals are evidently not yet wired otherwise they would not be down, or "off" in railway parlance, both at the same time. Signal box beyond bridge on the right side, whilst a makeshift scaffolding on a wagon enables the men to mount a trough-shaped girder under the roadway. The signals are of typical North British lattice type with pear-shaped spectacles at the ends of the arms. The lower oil lamps visible belong to the top arms, being wound up and down for maintenance by means of a windlass. A classic oil station platform lamp can be seen behind man's head on left.

engineering works, especially on the north side, and they were very costly to construct. The Forth Bridge Railway Company undertook only two sections: the south approach, which ran for some 1200 yards from the bridge arches, and the north approach, which ran for nearly two miles to join the North British line at Inverkeithing, a metal plate marking the boundary on the station platform there. The remaining connections were built by the North British: on the south side this consisted of a more direct route to Edinburgh, joining the Glasgow line at Saughton, and the line which branched westwards, which consisted of about 1000 yards of track from the Bridge to Winchburgh, as previously mentioned. The North British also built Dalmeny Station, which was originally called Forth Bridge Station.

Above: Burntisland—extension to the Docks on 1 April 1890.
Left: Glenfarg station under construction in April 1890.

A rare photograph of the now Dalmeny Station, still largely unaltered. The original name lasted only weeks.

Train Services

Traffic Facilities create traffic.
  —Railwayman's axiom

A table of comparative distances between Edinburgh and towns north of the Forth was published in an engineering journal of 1890. It compared those of the North British Railway, which was about to use both Forth and Tay Bridges, with those of the Caledonian Railway overland.

	N.B.R.	C.R.
Edinburgh - Aberdeen	130 miles	159 miles
Edinburgh - Dundee	59 ”	90 ”
Edinburgh - Montrose	90 ”	123 ”
Edinburgh - Perth	48 ”	69 ”

The paragraph went on to state that it was possible that an arrangement might be made for a train service from London to Perth in 9¾ hours, Dundee in 10½ hours and Aberdeen in 12¼ hours.

A study of the passenger train speeds between Edinburgh and London during the last century shows that the timings were unnecessarily leisurely. This was in part due to the safety consciousness of the traffic departments, who had to be especially vigilant for hazards to safety, given the standards of materials in use at the time, and the lack of reliable emergency automatic braking certainly in the earlier decades. Forty miles an hour was considered a quite acceptable average speed by the London and North-Western Company, as any speed in excess of this on a long run would greatly add to the expense.

In 1860 it took 16 hours to reach Euston from Aberdeen overnight, and 18½ hours during the day. From Kings Cross, anyone catching the 9.15p.m. would not reach Aberdeen until 4p.m. the following day. Only First Class passengers travelled in through carriages without having to change train *en route:* all other classes of passenger had to change trains a few times. Gradually these times were reduced, and on 1st November, 1887, the East Coast companies decided to take Third Class passengers on their 10a.m. "Flying Scotsman", to reach Edinburgh in 9 hours. Since it had been the policy of the West Coast companies to carry Third Class passengers on their 10-hour 10a.m. from Euston, they had to speed up their service, with the result that in 1888 the two factions started racing each other to Edinburgh.

THE GREAT RACE

By the end of that year Edinburgh could be reached in under 8 hours, Perth in 11 and Aberdeen in just under 14, but here the directors of the East Coast companies (the Great Northern and the North Eastern) baulked. They decided that 8½ hours was fast enough to complete the Edinburgh run: any faster would be unsafe and too costly. They abandoned the racing. The result of this voluntary restriction was that when the Forth Bridge was opened in 1890 they soon discovered that the shortened route to the north was no advantage to them: the West Coast companies (the London and North-Western and the Caledonian) had introduced an express the year before which could reach Aberdeen in 12 hours and 50 minutes, beating their rivals by half an hour.

About this time the Post Office considered sending mail north by whichever service was the quicker. Still the directors of the Eastern companies would not lift their speed restriction. The West Coast companies had the

contract anyway and held it until 1895. In June that year the managers of the Eastern companies at last reconsidered their restrictive policy. The Caledonian Railway had announced that its train from Carlisle would connect without fail with the Great North of Scotland's 8.05a.m. service northwards from Aberdeen. This meant arriving in Aberdeen at 7.40a.m., only five minutes behind the North British's East Coast service. The directors of the latter company came to the conclusion that it could neither reduce the weight of its rolling stock nor cut out any stops *en route* to decrease their time: the only hope was to reduce the time it took to reach Edinburgh from the South. The speed embargo was finally lifted, and on July 1st, 1895, the 8p.m. from Kings Cross reached Waverley in just over 8 hours, and steamed into Aberdeen at 7.20a.m.

To counter this new threat from the East Coast, the West Coast decided to reduce the load on their train in order to keep time, and in addition announced without prior notice that their 8p.m. train on July 15th would arrive in Aberdeen at 7a.m. the next morning.

The race was on with a vengeance, and during 1895 it attracted much enthusiastic attention from the public. A contemporary account was published in *"Kinnaber or The Great Railway Race of 1895"* by W.J. Scott, and he summarised the event in four stages:

	West Coast	East Coast
July 15th-21st	11 hrs	11 hrs 20 mins
July 22nd-28th	10 hrs 35 mins	10 hrs 45 mins
July 29th-Aug 18th	10 hrs 20 mins	10 hrs 25 mins
Aug 19th-22nd	9 hrs 35 mins	9 hrs 13 mins

The races culminated in a spectacular "exhibition run" by the West Coast companies who clocked up a time of 8 hours and 32 minutes with a 68-ton lightweight train carrying only a handful of passengers, employing two firemen, and omitting a

46

VII.—THE OUTCOME OF THIRTY-FIVE YEARS' COMPETITION.

In 1860 the best time to PERTH was 12h. 27m., & to ABERDEEN, 16h. 5m. (W.C.)

In 1878—PERTH, 11h. 25m.	ABERDEEN, 15h. 50m. (W.C.)
,, 11h. 25m.	,, 16h. 10m. (E.C.)
,, 1887— ,, 11h. 0m.	,, 13h. 55m. (W.C.)
,, (same time by E.C.)	,, (same time by E.C.)
,, 1889— ,, 10h. 15m.	,, 12h. 50m. (W.C.)
The E.C. route (E.C. 10h. 45m.)	,, (E.C. 13h. 20m.
was then by	
Larbert and the	
Caledonian Railway.	
In 1890—PERTH 9h. 55m.	,, 12h. 15m. (E.C.)
,, 9h. 57m.	,, 12h 20m. (W.C.)
(Forth Bridge opened.)	
In 1891—PERTH 9h. 45m.	,, 11h. 45m. (E.C.)
,, 1892— ,, same.	,, same. (E.C.)
,, 9h. 50m.	,, Same as in '91. (W.C.)
,, 1893— ,, 9h. 40m.	,, 11h. 35m. (E.C.)
,, 1894— ,, 9h. 40m.	,, 11h. 50m. (W.C.)
June, 1895— ,, Same as '94 (both routes) ,,	Same as in '94.
July 1st, 1895 ,, 9h. 20m.	,, 11h. 20m. (E.C.)
,, 9h. 30m.	,, 11h. 40m. (W.C.)
Then the RACE	11h. 20m. (E.C.)
,, 15th, 1895 ,, 9h. 5m. (W.C.) ,,	11h. 0m. (W.C.)
Sep. 1st, 1895 8h. 40m.	,, 10h. 25m. (E.C.)
(After the Race) 8h. 44m.	,, 10h. 30m. (W.C.)

So much for the worth of competition ; Inverness is now only 13¼ hours from London, Peterhead 13, and Elgin 13¼.

A table reproduced from Scott's KINNABER.
For comparison the Inter-City 125 THE
ABERDONIAN with four stops runs from
King's Cross to Aberdeen in 7hrs. 26 mins.
B.R. Timetables 1980-1981.

77

scheduled stop at Stirling. Such a run could not, of course, be offered as part of a regular service: it was uneconomical, impractical and dangerous. But it made the point about what could be achieved.

After the racing the East Coast resumed its timetable of July 28th, leaving Kings Cross at 8p.m. and arriving in Aberdeen at 6.45 the following morning. The West Coast kept their special service going and made it their regular 8p.m. run, but they detained the train at Crewe, so that it arrived in Aberdeen five minutes behind the East Coast train.

It is understandable that the companies should have relapsed into their old ways so far as the speeds of services were concerned. What is less undestandable from a modern viewpoint is why they did so little to improve on other aspects of the service. Some important stations in the country were on the whole hopelessly inadequate. By 1890 Waverley Station almost beggared description, even by contemporaries who were used to inadequate facilities. Although having three times the volume of traffic passing through it, the station had not been improved since the 1860's, and even then (in the '60's) it had been inadequate to meet the demands placed upon it with its higgledy-piggledy, end-to-end layout. It was a dirty, cramped and depressing warren.

In 1899 E. Foxwell wrote of the North British Railway Company:

> Here is a company whose handling of expresses sheds anything but lustre on the Scottish nation. On the platforms of Waverley Station at Edinburgh may be witnessed every evening in summer a scene of confusion so chaotic that a sober description of it is incredible to those who have not themselves survived it. Trains of caravan length come in portentously late from Perth, so that each is mistaken for another: these have to be broken up and remade on insufficient sidings, while bewildered crowds of tourists sway up and down amongst equally bewildered porters on the narrow village platform reserved for these most important expresses; the higher officials stand lost in subtle thought, returning now and then to repeated inquiries some masterpiece of reply couched in the cautious conditional, while the hands of the clock with a humourous air survey the abandoned sight, till at length, without any obvious reason and with sudden stealth, the shame-stricken driver hurries his packed passengers off into the dark.

Such conditions were by no means restricted to Edinburgh. In 1890 W.M. Acworth noted that many major stations were little better than shanties, and that the original Edinburgh and Glasgow terminus had not been re-painted since it was opened in 1842! He went on further to say that if the North British—which had declared in its prospectus of 1843 to "avoid all useless expense in ornamental works at stations and otherwise"—did not improve the shambolic situation: "an additional ten minutes at Waverley will take all the taste of the Forth Bridge out of the mouth of the most enthusiastic traveller". Writing at the same time, J.Pearson Pattinson said that the runnings of the Edinburgh suburban line were "so irregular as to be quite a curiosity".

The late John Thomas, the modern railway historian, states that the principal waiting room at Waverley was sixteen feet square, which was incidentally the same size as the Black Hole of Calcutta—with a main departure platform only four feet wide. Traffic which arrived from the Forth Bridge had to queue up from Saughton Junction, often for as long as an hour, before a platform became available. Hapless passengers who were travelling South would arrive at Waverley hopelessly late, and many had to stay overnight in Edinburgh because they had missed their connections.

The modern traveller is accustomed to interminable delays in airport lounges, but how much worse it must have been for the nineteenth-century rail traveller, cooped up in a motionless, unheated train. In 1890, with

The most impressive locomotive ever to run on the Forth Bridge, was the London & North Eastern Railway's P2 class which was built at Doncaster in 1934. "Cock o' the North" was the first of a class of six engines and when new she went to France for experimental work on the famous locomotive testing plant at Vitry near Paris. A few runs between Paris and Tours were followed by her exhibition alongside a French Pacific 4-6-2 at the Gare du Nord before returning home.

The eight-coupled 6ft. 2ins. wheel arrangement was advocated, not without reason at the time, to improve hauling capacity with one engine on the hilly main line to Aberdeen where the heavier trains with third class sleeping cars added often well exceeded 500 tons, too much for the Pacifics to keep time.

All six engines differed from each other in detail, and although very successful when new, in spite of misgivings in some official quarters as to the performance of the long wheelbase on sharp curves, the class as a whole seemed to prove costly in maintenance later on, and ere the war was over they had been rebuilt and simplified to the 4-6-2 wheel arrangement.

North British Railway 4-4-2 Atlantic HAZELDEAN on a
Perth Express coming off the Forth Bridge. An undated photograph
by G.H. Soole. This locomotive was withdrawn by the London &
North Eastern Railway in 1936.

the exception of a few First Class long-distance through coaches or private family saloons, there were no lavatories available. This serious inconvenience was never mentioned by Victorian writers discussing railway journeys, even in the handbooks which proliferated at the beginning and indeed throughout the railway age, and which purported to tell all that the reader needed to know about railway travel. Travelling by train must have been an ordeal, and in Britain we were singularly slow to provide universal sanitation and proper heating and lighting for railway passengers. Consequently many people still preferred to travel by sea.

Railway companies, and the North British Railway Company in particular, tended to receive a thoroughly bad press: to judge by the comments of the time, many people began to wonder whether the Great Bridge had really been worth it.

Railway Traffic On The Forth Bridge

The volume of traffic on the Forth Bridge continued to grow after its first year of operation, when some £22,000 extra revenue was taken from passengers and parcels: over 20,000 passengers and 8,000 goods trains crossed the Bridge during the first financial year. By 1900, the ghastliness of the old Waverley Station was a thing of the past. Its rebuilding, together with the completion of additional approach lines and extra tunnelling to the east and west of the city, led to considerable increase in local train services. North of the Forth the new lines opened up the Fife resorts and a new direct route to Perth.

From a national point of view, however, the Bridge could not benefit travellers from the south all that much without a faster service to Edinburgh during the day. A brief description of the evolution of Anglo-Scottish train services and its importance in the functioning of the Forth Bridge is perhaps worthwhile.

The races of 1895 were really stunts which were not meant to establish a timetable for future Anglo-Scottish traffic, were considered by both sides to be costly feats, awkward to run between local and goods traffic, not feasible in adverse weather conditions, and last but not least possibly dangerous. Accordingly an agreement was reached in June 1896 for a minimum 8½ hour daytime schedule for services between London and Edinburgh and London and Glasgow. Overnight journeys were still performed for some months after the races at speeds which were not to be equalled for another forty years.

The East Coast companies, using the Forth and Tay Bridges, reached Aberdeen overnight in 10 hours and 25 minutes from London whilst the West Coast train arrived 5 minutes later. However, on July 13th, 1896, the 8p.m. from Euston derailed itself on a curve at Preston due to excessive speed (50 mph instead of 10mph!) and an agreed deceleration by the two sides followed, the effect of which was to discourage speeding between England and Scotland until the 1930's.

In 1897 the overnight train from Kings Cross to Edinburgh took 7 hours and 45 minutes for the trip but although the day timetable was 8½ hours, the day trains seemed incapable of being punctual. *The History of the North British Railway* by John Thomas tells us that during 1898 the second portion of the "Flying Scotsman" which left Waverley at 10.07a.m. had an average late arrival at Kings Cross of 10.27 minutes in July, 22.17 minutes in August and 33.84 minutes in September. This particular train had apparently a total of 1,711 minutes against it. In the reverse direction things were no better, with the result that the North British were not at all pleased when they had to run specials to places north and west of Edinburgh for passengers who had missed connections due to late arrivals from the south. To make matters worse the NBR had to bear all the extra cost.

The East Coast arrangements had always been for the Great Northern Railway to work the through trains from London to York, and for the North Eastern to work them from York on to Edinburgh. The North British were not allowed to work the through expresses over their own line between Berwick and Edinburgh owing to an Act of Parliament which had been in force since 1862, imposing this sanction in return for the NBR being allowed to run their local Border trains into Newcastle from Hexham. Such running powers were very numerous between the old railway companies although all were not exercised. So the NE and the NB agreement was nothing new but it caused trouble and bickering such as occurs nowadays between an ill-assorted landlord and tenant wed to each other by the Rent Acts.

Although on the face of things the alliance between the East Coast companies appeared amicable when fighting the West Coast common enemy, the public only became aware of the acrimony when things came to a head and were aired in the courts, and eventually in the House of Lords. Much of the trouble stemmed from timing between York and Edinburgh, the North Eastern's over-borrowing of North British banking engines, and the stopping of NE trains on NB territory in order to help themselves to NB water. Eventually the NB tired of the situation and

started to run its own engines between Edinburgh and Berwick, really by force of occupation, which resulted in a court case before the Railway and Canal Commissioners in January 1897. The court found that the NB used two locomotives when the NE only needed one and a compromise whereby the services were divided between the two sides was settled. However, this compromise did not come into effect for a few months, and even then the intentions of the judgement were not properly implemented.

Behaviour between the two companies continued to be decidedly churlish. The NE, for example, established its own booking office at Waverley and refused to allow Berwick passengers on their trains if they held tickets bought from the NB. And so it went on. They even played the fool with each other's time-tables by holding up trains through signal checks. Eventually, though, the North Eastern regained power and the North British gave up the struggle.

Another landmark was the introduction of dining cars between London and Scotland. These had been in use on the afternoon services since 1893, but in 1898 the West Coast put one on their Glasgow to London morning run and cut out their 20 minutes refreshment stop at Preston. They did not take the 20 minutes off the running time however, using them instead to ease the overall schedule. In so doing they began to improve their time-keeping. In any case they were adhering to the 8½ hour agreement. The equivalent 20 minutes stop on the opposite coast was at York, where the NE did the catering. In an effort to shorten the overall time between London and Edinburgh, the NE first suggested cutting the York stop by 10 minutes then grudgingly agreed to have a dining car on the "Flying Scotsman" provided that the 20 minutes saved was taken off the journey time. From December 1900 a quarter of an hour was taken off the Anglo-Scottish runs, reducing the times by mutual consent to

An old stereo photograph. The method of laying the rails is well illustrated.

94   CAMERON'S GUIDE—EDINBURGH EXHIBITION, 1890.

CAMERON'S PENNY GUIDES,

Expressly written for this Series, contain accurate and more full information than in **some** others six times the price.   Large Type, Illustrated, in Covers.

EDINBURGH CITY.

ENVIRONS OF EDINBURGH.
Viz., Dalkeith, Hawthornden, Roslin, South Queensferry, Aberdour, Burntisland, etc.

MELROSE, ABBOTSFORD,
Dryburgh Abbey, etc.

GLASGOW, ETC.

AYR AND DUMFRIES,
The Land of Burns.

STIRLING AND THE FORTH,
Bannockburn, Bridge of Allan, Dunblane, etc.

ALSO JUST PUBLISHED,

THE FORTH BRIDGE

AND ALL ABOUT IT TO DATE

PRICE ONE PENNY EACH.   Per Post, 1½d.   The Seven, **9d.**

EXTRACTS FROM NEWSPAPER NOTICES.

Scotsman says :—"A cheap and handy pamphlet, containing a readable account."
Edinburgh Evening News says :—" The average reader will find it simply invaluable. . . . Visitors who wish to obtain an intelligible grasp of the famous structure **cannot do** better than furnish themselves with a copy."
Glasgow Evening Times says :—"An excellent pennyworth."

EDINBURGH : Published by J. A. CAMERON & CO., 21 ELDER STREET, and may be had at the Railway Bookstalls, from most News-Agents, and at the News-Box, 4 Princes Street.

GLASGOW—W. LOVE, 226 Argyle Street.

AYR—At the Railway Bookstall.   MELROSE—... M'BEAN, Bookseller.
STIRLING—D. MILLAR & SON, 39 King St. │ PORTOBELLO—A. TAYLOR, 89 High St.

CAMERON'S A-B-C EDINBURGH
PENNY TIME-TABLES

Showing at a glance How and When to go from Edinburgh to the different Stations in Scotland, and the principal ones in England, and Return, with the Fares, etc.

SIMPLE AND CORRECT.   EASY AS A-B-C.
A CHILD CAN UNDERSTAND.

CONTENTS.

Arrangement of Stations ; Cab Fares and Bye-Laws ; Cars (Tramway) ; City and Country Omnibuses ; Edinburgh—What to See and How ; Through Routes ; Steamers, &c.

INSTRUCT YOUR NEWS-AGENT TO SEND IT MONTHLY.

Cost—ONE SHILLING per Year.

EDINBURGH : Published by J. A. CAMERON & CO., 21 ELDER STREET; and may be had at the Railway Bookstalls, from most News-Agents, and at the News-Box, 4 Princes Street.

Above: Example of the first references to the Forth Bridge in guide books and timetables.

64   CAMERON'S GUIDE—EDINBURGH EXHIBITION, 1890.

R. URE, Florist, Fine Art Pottery, &c.

(Court 1, Main Building, Stand No. 484, measuring 250 feet, Edinburgh Exhibition, 1890.)

BOUQUETS and **FLORAL BASKETS** as made by us to Their Royal Highnesses The Prince and Princess of Wales, the Princesses Louise, Victoria, and Maud of Wales, &c., &c.

THE CHOICEST BOUQUETS, WREATHS, and CROSSES. at all Seasons.

ART POTTERY AND FERN BOWLS,

Largest and most Choice Selection in Scotland—specially imported from the most Celebrated Potteries in the World.

Many of the Designs are our own, and cannot be obtained elsewhere.

City Address :—R. URE, Rutland Corner, Princes Street, Edinburgh.

FRUITS, FLOWERS, AND FINE ART POTTERY.

THE FORTH BRIDGE'S RIVAL.

—— THE WORLD'S WONDER. ——

The Best, Largest, and Most Substantial Washing Shirt in Scotland.

VIZ :—

THE FORTH BRIDGE SHIRT

PRICE 2/9. Can only be had at

W. JOHNSTON'S, 63 HIGH STREET,

BEST KNOWN AS

JOHNSTON'S, the Cheap or Busy Wholesale Price Shop.

HAVE THE LARGEST SHIRT TRADE IN EDINBURGH.

ALSO,

All Classes of Drapery, Clothing, Hats and Caps. Hosiery, Millinery, and Smallwares, etc.—all at Wholesale Prices.

THE TRADE SUPPLIED.

Note Address—

W. JOHNSTON,

63 HIGH STREET, EDINBURGH

(*Adjoining John Knox's House*).

For Really Good Photos. at Moderate Prices

GO TO

FRED E. BAILEY,

92, 96 NICOLSON STREET, EDINBURGH.

F. E. BAILEY guarantees satisfaction to all his Patrons.

PHOTOS. of CHILDREN *and* GROUPS *most successfully produced.*

The Forth Bridge even had a shirt named after it!

85

 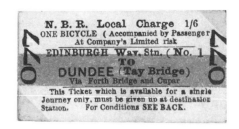 

Some samples of early tickets relevant to the story of the Forth Railway Bridge.

8¼ hours—but not before the East Coast companies had had another row between themselves. At any rate, the introduction of dining cars finally did away with the awful scramble for, and the bolting of, hot food in the station refreshment rooms.

In 1901 the Midland Railway and the North British accelerated their 9.30a.m. from St. Pancras to Waverley via Carlisle to arrive at 6.05p.m., ten minutes in front of their rivals to Edinburgh. Both had left London at 10a.m. However, they found that they could not keep time subsequently, and the "Flying Scotsman" from Kings Cross started arriving a bit early so as not to be outdone. In the meantime the West Coast trains had more often than not been arriving late at the Caledonian Railway's Princes Street Station in Edinburgh, so they had decided that something just simply had to be done. To everyone's astonishment one day the West Coast train arrived in Edinburgh 35 minutes early. The press anticipated another race, but nothing developed and the companies went back to their 8¼ hour agreement, in which

incidentally, the Midland route was never a partner. The timetables remained virtually unchanged until the 1914-18 war, during which time of course everything deteriorated. When the war was over, the 10a.m. from King's Cross was taking 9 hrs 50 mins to Edinburgh, and one could not get to Aberdeen in the daytime from London. There was no morning service from Euston to Glasgow or Edinburgh, but there was an 8.50a.m. to Glasgow from St. Pancras by Midland Railway, taking 10 hours 40 mins.

By the summer of 1923 the 8¼ hours daytime schedule was resumed but the railway companies were gradually being transformed. The East Coast companies, for instance, were amalgamated with others to form the London and North Eastern Railway, and the West Coast had joined to form the London Midland and Scottish. Various experiments were made in non-stop running but as the 8¼ hour timetables still persisted, it became necessary to look to the passenger's comfort: various distractions, such as cocktail bars, hair-dressing salons, Ladies' retiring rooms, cinema

Forth Bridge

17/7/03. As our landlady can't put up over Sunday, we are leaving by N13 train tomorrow afternoon for home. We have had three days of rain and are getting tired of it.

The Forth Bridge from N.W.   EDINBURGH.   "Cockburn Hotel"

I went under this Bridge yesterday 24th Aug (1903) afternoon

1051. in a steamer. Sydney McNeill

Top: A view from South Queensferry published by the Reliable Series in black and white. Card posted from Edinburgh in 1903.   *Bottom: Black and white example published by Hartmann and posted 1903.*

The Stanley-Butler Steamship Co., Ltd.

Registered Office: **190, HIGH STREET.**

Proprietors of Saloon Pleasure Steamer Services on Firth of Forth.

Daily Sailings from West Pier, Leith. **Special Cruisers** arranged for Parties of 50 and upwards

The Forth Bridge, the greatest triumph of modern engineering, begun in 1882, took seven year's to construct, and during these years gave employment to an average of 3,500 men. Its chief dimensions are—total length, upwards of 1½ miles; depth over piers 342 or 361 feet above mean tide; diameter of largest Tubes, 12 feet; width of spans over fairways, nearly 1,700 feet; total amount of steel over 50,000 tons; wind pressure allowed for, 56lls. per square foot; greatest depth of water in channels, 218 feet; contraction and expansion, between 6 and 7 feet, or 10 inches per 1,000 feet; total cost, £3,500,000.

An example of a business card in black and white and unused. The printed address appears to have been incomplete and to have been finished off with a typewriter.

coaches and wireless sets were tried out, but as Hamilton Ellis wrote ". . . at an average speed of 47.6 mph, in the course of which you longed for the engine to break down, or for someone to fall out, or for an aeroplane to crash on the track—anything, however drastic, to break that interminable rumble."

Eventually, in 1932, it was decided to speed up the daytime services from London to Scotland. 25 minutes was taken off the winter "Flying Scotsman" and 45 minutes off the summer non-stop. The "Royal Scot" took 20 minutes off in winter and 35 minutes in summer. Mild unofficial racing appeared to be starting again in spite of parings in the timetables. In May, 1936, the L.M.S. ran from Euston to Glasgow Central in 7 hours 35 minutes, to which the L.N.E.R. replied with 7 hours 25 minutes from Kings Cross to Waverley. During the summer the "Flying

Scotsman" took 7¼ hours non-stop to Edinburgh, so that Aberdeen was reached in 10 hours 28 minutes.

The average daytime train services to Scotland from London had quickened by three quarters of an hour from the First World War to early 1937, but the night trains had slowed down by almost the same margin. On July 5th of that year, however, new fast streamlined services were inaugurated to Scotland, the L.N.E.R. offering a six-hour Coronation summer service from Kings Cross to Waverley and the L.M.S. replying with a 6½ hour Coronation Scot service to Glasgow. So the competition was still there some fifty years after the first railway races. What was not realised then was that it was really the apogee of the steam age in Britain. After World War Two, nationalisation was to preclude all railway competition.

The four-in-hand bound for the Forth Bridge featured on a postcard from the "Edinburgh at the Turn of the Century" series published by Edinburgh City Libraries. Tickets for the four-in-hand were purchased from McLaren's Booking Office at number three Princes Street. A stop was made at Cramond Brig for five minutes, and then for an hour on arrival at the Hawes, South Queensferry. In 1902 the fare was one shilling (5 new pence). The driver wore a red coat.

REASONS

FOR TRAVELLING
BY THE . . . .

NORTH BRITISH RAILWAY.

● ● ●

BECAUSE THE N.B.R.

Is the most extensive System in Scotland.

Encircles and intersects the whole of romantic Scotland.

Directly serves the districts rich in **History, Poetry, Tradition, Romance** and **Legend.**

Is famed for speed, comfort, punctuality, and safety.

Is the direct and only route to—

The Home and Haunts of Sir Walter Scott and the Historic Borderland ;

Melrose Station for Melrose Abbey, and Abbotsford ;

St. Boswells Station for Dryburgh Abbey ;

Selkirk for the Vales of Ettrick and Yarrow and St. Mary's Loch.

Takes you to Silloth (on the Solway Firth) a delightful Seaside Resort, for Steamers to Douglas (Isle of Man), and Dublin.

Takes you to North Berwick, Gullane, Dunbar, and the other **East Coast** Seaside Golfing Resorts.

Takes you by the **World Renowned Forth Bridge** to **St. Andrews**, Crail, Elie, Leven, Burntisland, Aberdour, and other **Fifeshire** Seaside Golfing Resorts.

Takes you by the Forth and Tay Bridges to **Dundee**, Arbroath, Montrose, Stonehaven, **Aberdeen**, Balmoral, and all parts of the Great North of Scotland Railway System.

Takes you by **Forth Bridge** to Dunfermline, **Stirling**, and Perth, thence to **Inverness**, Strathpeffer, Nairn, Wick and all parts of the **Highland Railway** System.

Takes you to all the most **attractive Golf Courses** in Scotland.

Takes you to all the **famous** Watering Resorts on **both sides** of the **Firth of Forth**, noted for Bracing Air, Splendid Bathing, Boating and Sea-fishing.

Takes you to **Inverkeithing** for the Naval Base.

Takes you *via* **West Highland Railway**, through Unrivalled Mountain, Moor, and Loch Scenery, to Glencoe, Oban, Fort William, for Ben Nevis, Glen Nevis.

Takes you to **Fort Augustus**, thence by **Steamer** through Loch Ness to **Inverness.**

Takes you to **Bonnie Prince Charlie's** and Clanranald's **Country**, Loch Eil, **Loch Shiel.** The Falls of Morar, Arisaig, and **Mallaig**, thence by **Steamers** to Skye, Lewis, and the other **Western Islands.**

Takes you to **Aberfoyle**, for Loch Ard, **Loch Lomond** (for Ben Lomond), **Loch Katrine** and the **Trossachs** (Rob Roy's Country).

Takes you to **Craigendoran Pier** (Helensburgh), thence by a fleet of fast and commodious **Steamers** to Loch Long, Holy Loch, **Dunoon**, Rothesay, Kyles of **Bute**, and all the other **lovely Lochs** and charming watering **Places** on the **Firth of Clyde.**

Has direct connection to and from places in England, served by the **East Coast** and **Midland Routes.**

Takes you to **every place worth seeing** in Scotland, England, and the **Continent.**

Apply to Mr D. Deuchars, Superintendent of the Line, Waverley Station, Edinburgh, for Travel Publications enumerated on pages 2 and 3.

☞ **Will you kindly hand this Pamphlet to a friend after you are done with it.**

General Manager,
Edinburgh.

W. F. JACKSON.

The Popular Corridor Restaurant Car Express crossing the World renowned Forth Bridge *en route* to the famous Fifeshire Resorts, Aberdeen and the North

THE North British Railway System is the most extensive in Scotland. It encircles and intersects the whole of picturesque Scotland, and directly serves the districts rich in History, Poetry, Tradition, Romance and Legend. The varied Scenery, especially that opened up by the West Highland and Invergarry and Fort Augustus Railways, is without rival in this country. Almost in every district will be found Picturesque Lochs and Bays, Silvery Rivers, Loftiest Bens, Historic Glens. It also provides convenient and expeditious Through Communication with all parts of the United Kingdom.

Melrose Abbey

Important Notice to Tourists.

The Direct and **Only Route** to the Home and Haunts of Sir Walter Scott and the Historic Borderland, is by **North British Railway.** Therefore, to avoid inconvenience and delay, ask for Tickets *via* "Waverley Route," which extends from Newcastle (*via* Hexham) in the East, and Carlisle in the South, to Edinburgh (Waverley Station).

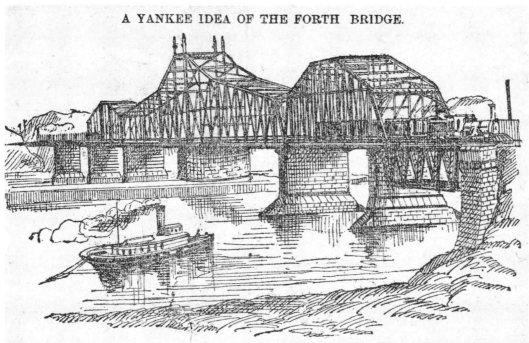

A YANKEE IDEA OF THE FORTH BRIDGE.

As it is always interesting to see ourselves or our work as others see us, we reproduce from the *New York World* the subjoined sketch of "the great structure thrown over the Forth in Scotland." It is described as "an English rival of Brooklyn Bridge," and, like the golf illustrations we published some time ago, the present sketch has evidently been evolved from the brain of some imaginative Yankee after listening to a description.

Above: The Evening Dispatch provides an 1890's American vision of the Bridge for the amusement of its readers.
Opposite left: A leaflet in the author's collection includes the Forth Bridge among its illustrations. Mr. Deuchars operated at the Waverley prior to the First World War, when railways were in their heyday and were practically the only means by which the population could travel. The absence of a telephone number for applications can be noted.

FORTH BRIDGE HOTEL.

WITH COMPLIMENTS.

Valentines Series 47483

Hawes' Hotel, Queensferry

Top: a view of the Bridge looking north, probably in the 1920s.
Rare to have people included as here. Unused specimen by Judges
Ltd of Hastings. Top right: The Forth Bridge Hotel. Bottom: The
Hawes Hotel.

7

A SYMBOL FOR SCOTLAND

The impact of the Bridge was immense—not only did it open up the fastest railway route to the north of Scotland, but more importantly it became a national symbol of progress. It was universally hailed as a masterpiece of heavy engineering, with some commentators going as far as to call it the eighth Wonder of the World. All who saw the Bridge, and there were thousands who made the crossing for the sole purpose of admiring the workmanship, were impressed by the stark magnificence of the structure. Even in an age of dynamic industrial expansion it was soon realised that the Bridge had established an unsurpassable standard, and that it represented the supreme achievement of Victorian engineering. Never again would a situation lend itself, nor men of sufficient ability and resolve be found, to build anything to rival it.

The Bridge so captured the Victorian imagination because it was a manifestation of their most devoutly held belief, that through hard work, grim determination and the employment of the most advanced techniques, man was capable of anything, capable even of subjugating nature.

In many ways the Bridge symbolised the spirit of the age. To some, albeit few, that idea was anathema and the Bridge represented all that was ugly, brutal, industrial and progressive. Particularly vocal amongst those who found the Bridge deeply offensive was the famous art critic and historian John Ruskin who so hated the Bridge and all it stood for that he regularly included it in his lectures. He believed that "the most beautiful things in the world are the most useless; peacocks and lilies for instance" and when confronted by the awesome practicality of the Bridge he said to the audience that having seen it he "wished he had been born a blind fish in a Kentucky cave".

Ironically it was another, equally distinguished, art critic and historian, Sir Kenneth Clark (now Lord Clark) who elevated the Bridge into the realms of High Art when he included a photograph of it on the back cover of his classic work *Civilisation*. What Ruskin saw as the crass practicality of the Bridge, a cathedral built to honour the worst aspects of industrialism, Clark saw as an elegant monument to Victorian pragmatism that with its soaring girders more effectively captured the essence of the age than any other building or structure created during those extraordinarily productive years.

For less rarified citizens than Mr Ruskin and Sir Kenneth Clark, the Bridge became an important institution. Naturally the Bridge was a boon to travellers, but it was not for this reason that it so gripped the popular imagination. Like the Eiffel Tower the Forth Railway Bridge was far greater than the sum of its parts, so that it was never just another bridge, nor was it even "the" Bridge—but a mythic, fantastic bridge.

Perhaps one of the greatest tributes to the Forth Rail Bridge—and certainly one it is hard to improve upon—came from C. Hamilton Ellis in his *North British Railway* history published in 1955:

Since then this superb bridge has stridden the Firth of Forth, changeless in a changing world, tremendous, most grandly austere. Its beauty is unconscious, as in so many Victorian

Earthenware plate, 9½" diameter.

structures. Not one of its designers, builders or sponsors remarked on any ornamental quality, yet there it stands in all its giant grace, today a part of the land-and-seascape on which it was imposed, and scenically as full of moods as a mountain. It should be seen at sunrise; it should be seen in the evening; it should be seen in a storm; it should be seen when a white sea mist drifts up the firth, hiding all but the tops of the towers; it should be seen at night, when the fireman of a crossing engine opens his firedoor and floods the girders momentarily with an orange glare up to the topmost booms. To sailors in two great wars it has been one of the best-loved landmarks in Great Britain. It is a lovely bridge.

As has already been mentioned, thousands made the crossing for no other reason than to say they had done so. From the earliest days it became considered lucky to throw pennies out of the train window when crossing the Bridge, as if those colossal girders were imbued with magical properties, casting a spell over the travellers who used it. Each train was alive with small boys, their faces eagerly pressed to the windows; and no matter at what hour of the day or night the crossing was made travellers would sit up and take notice. Some would mark their respect with hushed reverence, others with quiet comment and the more flamboyant with whoops of excitement as they threw their pennies.

Messrs Fowler, Baker and Arrol can hardly have imagined the influence the Bridge was to exert on Scottish life. From the very outset of building it had attracted an enormous amount of attention in the press, who were quick to realise that it was a subject which fascinated the public. Rumours about every aspect of the Bridge abounded and the public was rapacious in its appetite for facts—or fictions.

In 1896 the well known stunt man Tommy Burns announced to the world that he intended to dive from the Bridge, and asked permission of the Bridge Inspector. This was refused—but Burns insisted that he would make the dive nonetheless. In August of the same year he claimed that he had dived from the Bridge, having been rowed out to Inchgarvie by two witnesses. The Bridge authorities vigorously denied that he had done so—but they admitted that some trousers and a pair of shoes had been found near the track at the point where Burns claimed he had dived. It is uncertain which side of the story is true, but what is certain is that if he did successfully make the dive he was lucky to survive, for the following year he was killed in front of a crowd of 3,000 when diving off the end of Rhyl pier, which is 100 feet high. The Forth Rail Bridge reaches a height of 156 feet.

Over the years the Bridge has continued to make the news, and most often in a controversial manner. Perhaps naturally enough, one recurring question concerns the safety of the structure. A question at the half-yearly meeting of the North British Railway on 17 March, 1910 provides one example. There Mr. C.J. Thompson of Brampton in Cumberland asked:

> My Lord, the rumour has been current in the South of England that the speed of trains has been reduced on the Forth Bridge, and that trains have to stop at both ends of the Bridge. The reason given for this is, that the foundations of the Forth Bridge have sunk, and if this is so will you tell us to what appreciable extent. Another is that a flaw has been discovered in the Forth Bridge.

The Chairman, the Earl of Dalkeith, was not amused and replied in the most forthright terms:

> Mr. Thompson did not say where he heard the rumours or who invented or imagined them, but in answer to him, I may say that they are all purely imaginary. (Applause). The Forth Bridge, which does not of course belong to this Company, but to a separate Company, is in as perfect a state as it is possible for anything to be. The only truth in the matter is that there were some trains running over it at above speed, and in consequence a speed limit has

The Fleet protecting the Forth Bridge. A black and white card by D & S K which shows signs of having been touched up considerably.

Opposite: British official photograph: Crown copyright reserved. German bomber's view of 1939 attack on the Firth of Forth.

This photograph was taken by an enemy bomber during the Luftwaffe's first attack of the war on the British mainland, when on October 16, 1939, German aircraft unsuccessfully bombed naval units in the Firth of Forth. The Forth Bridge is easily identifiable, and the dark patches on the water indicate where bombs fell. It was recorded that the Germans interpreted the island of Inch Garvie in the photograph to be a direct hit on the bridge.

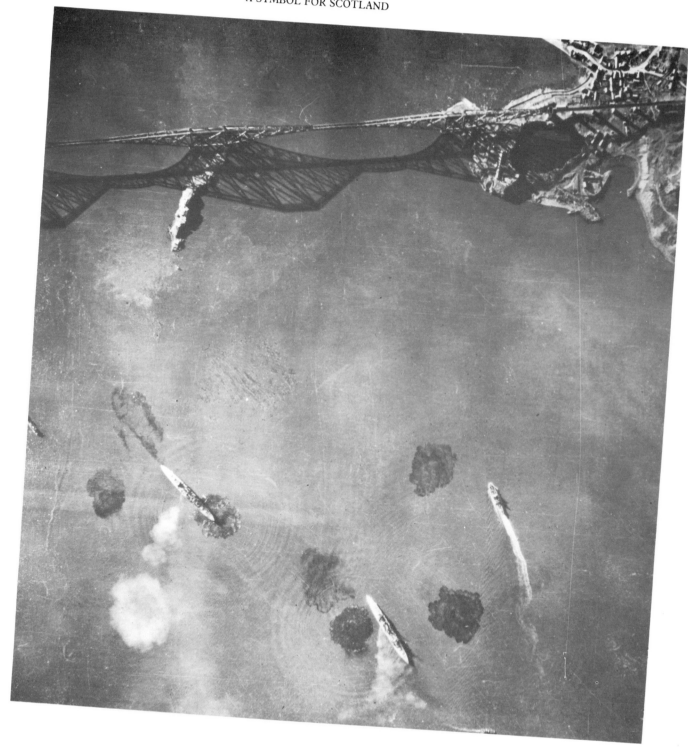

been fixed and is now in force; but there is absolutely nothing wrong with the structure. There is no engineering work in the whole world in better condition than the Forth Bridge. *(Applause).*

Even as recently as August, 1982, *The Scotsman* carried an article concerning fears by a Fife Region councillor, Dr. Peter Davison, about the "sadly dilapidated" condition of the Forth Railway Bridge. After a mission on the River Forth using binoculars from a boat, the councillor concluded that, "A key part of the Scottish transport system and an important part of Scotland's heritage is at risk". He expressed fears that if the Bridge was declared unsafe in a few years the loss-making railway line through Fife could justifiably be closed. Significantly perhaps, British Rail were emphatic that "there is no intention of closing the bridge which is structurally sound with a long-term future".

In a social historical sense the Bridge has also reflected the changing times it has experienced. The question of women on the Bridge reflects this well. At the turn of the century, for instance, when it was fashionable to walk across the Bridge, provided a permit could be obtained from the North British Railway Company, a letter from John Walker, the general manager, to the locomotive superintendent, Matthew Holmes, states:

> I have your letter of 21st inst. and send herewith the order to Mr. Hunter to admit Mr. C.M. Smith and two friends to the Forth Bridge. I presume that neither of the two friends is a lady, because we hesitate to allow ladies to walk across the bridge owing to the great danger there is to them, especially when express trains are passing.

The bridge engineer would usually justify objection to the presence of women on the Bridge because of their voluminous clothing on the narrow footways. Although the North British Railway never liked to say so on their permits, it was a case of 'gentlemen only' and 'no ladies' became an unwritten law. A significant breakthrough, then, was made when on 11th June, 1934, Miss E.O Culle, librarian in Washington of the Association of American Railroads—suitably attired in tight-fitting skirt and hat—walked across the Bridge at the invitation of the London and North Eastern Railway in Scotland.

Much of the news concerning the Bridge has also been dramatic; such as when it was the target for the first daylight bombing raid of the Second World War, on October 16th 1939. A German bomber separated from its squadron resolved to destroy it but fortunately failed to hit the Bridge itself and caused only slight damage to a ship passing underneath. Later in the war some barrage balloons flying above the Bridge were struck by lightning, caught fire and fell blazing onto the tender of a crossing train. Once again the Bridge had escaped damage.

There has never been a serious derailment on the Forth Bridge, and in spite of its location which experiences the fiercest gales imaginable only minor incidents have occurred. However, Mr Benzie who was signalman in charge of the North Queensferry box for many years told the author that on one occasion he had to stop a train because he saw some soldiers on the roof of a carriage. They had been to a T.A. camp and had started larking around. The escapade ended in disaster for one of the soldiers was decapitated.

But perhaps the most dramatic incident in the Bridge's history is entirely fictitious. In John Buchan's novel *The Thirty Nine Steps,* the innocent hero Richard Hannay is pursued by police to the North of Scotland when he is trapped just as the train is crossing the Forth Bridge and is forced to pull the communication cord and climb out of the compartment window onto the Bridge itself. He is followed, climbs through a manhole and hangs from a girder while his pursuers frantically search for him amongst the lattice work. The book has been filmed a few times, but the original pre-war version by the Master of Suspense, Alfred Hitchcock has not been bettered, and the scene on the Bridge may lay claim to being one of the more dramatic episodes in earlier film history.

The Bridge was further embedded into the popular consciousness by the frequency with which its image was reproduced by shrewd advertisers, who realised that by coupling their products, be they oatcakes or women's nylon stockings, with the Bridge the products concerned were given an instant pedigree that suggested to the potential purchaser he could expect the product to reflect the widely renowned sterling qualities of the Bridge itself.

In many ways the image of the Bridge transcended the practical importance. The mere representation of it, be it on postcard or souvenir, acted iconographically on the beholder. The importance of the Bridge as an icon should not be underestimated—for no matter how poor the representation, and there have been some extremely poor ones, the Bridge was instantly recognisable for being what it was and where it was. In the same way that representations of the Pyramids or the Statue of Liberty have come to symbolise the countries in which they stand—the Bridge sums up Scotland with all her sternness, her rugged beauty and her ingenuity.

BIBLIOGRAPHY

EXPRESS TRAINS ENGLISH AND FOREIGN. E. Foxwell. Stanford, 1884.

THE FORTH BRIDGE. W. Westhoven. Supplement to "Engineering", 1890.

THE FORTH BRIDGE. Supplement to "Industries", 1890.

THE FORTH RAILWAY BRIDGE. The Giant's Anatomy. Philip Phillips. R. Grant, Edinburgh, 1890.

THE RAILWAYS OF SCOTLAND. W. Acworth. John Murray, 1890.

THE BEST WAY THERE. W.J. Scott. The Railway Press Co., 1892.

KINNABER OR THE GREAT RAILWAY RACE OF 1895. W.J. Scott. Keagan Paul, Trench, Trubner & Co., 1897.

A HUNDRED YEARS OF INLAND TRANSPORT. C. Sherrington. Duckworth, 1934.

THE RAILWAY MANIA AND ITS AFTERMATH. H.G. Lewin, The Railway Gazette, 1936.

THE NORTH BRITISH RAILWAY. C. Hamilton Ellis. Ian Allan, 1955.

THE RAILWAY RACE TO THE NORTH. O.S. Nock. Ian Allan, 1958.

THE HIGH GIRDERS. The Story of the Tay Bridge Disaster. John Prebble. Secker & Warburg, 1956.

THE DICTIONARY OF NATIONAL BIOGRAPHY.

STATISTICAL ACCOUNT OF SCOTLAND.

THE RAILWAY MAGAZINE.

THE LOCOMOTIVE MAGAZINE.

THE JOURNAL OF THE STEPHENSON LOCOMOTIVE SOCIETY.

BRADSHAW'S GENERAL RAILWAY and STEAM NAVIGATION GUIDE.

GLOSSARY

ABERDOUR means "the mouth of" the Dour, which is a small stream which reaches the Forth below the village situated on the Fife coast. The old Parish of Aberdour originally belonged to the Monastery of Inchcolm which was founded by Alexander I in 1123. The Monastery was given lands in and around Aberdour by the Mortimer family in return for the privilege of being buried in the church. Their name persists in Mortimer's Deep, the stretch of water between Inchcolm and Aberdour. Most of the lands eventually came into the hands of the Earls of Morton and the Earls of Moray.

With the coming of the railway, the Fife Coast became much more of a holiday resort, and during the First War Aberdour was quite a social centre in season when Admiral Beatty had a house there. The quiet village atmosphere never left the area until the Forth Road Bridge was opened and the age of the motor car had disfigured the little place with litter, double yellow lines, traffic signals and building schemes.

ATAHUALPA died 1553. Last of the Incas. Captured by Pizarro and strangled when the Spaniards thought that he had double-crossed them over the arranging of an enormous ransom for his release.

BAILIE. In Scotland a magistrate elected by town councillors to preside in police or burgh courts.

BARLOW, WILLIAM HENRY, 1812-1902. Apprenticed at Woolwich Dockyard. Erected ordnance structures at Constantinople 1832-1838. Appointed Chief Engineer, Midland Railway 1844. Designed St Pancras Station, built 1862-1869. Consultant at Tay Bridge disaster enquiry. Designed new Tay Bridge 1882. President Institute Civil Engineers 1879-1880.

BEAUMONT EGG. A corruption of Beaumontage which is any material used for filling cracks in metal or woodwork, acceptable in some cases but not when used as a bluff to hide bad craftsmanship. Said to be called after Elie de Beaumont, the French geologist.

BLACKNESS CASTLE. By the Act of Union it was stipulated that the Castle should always be kept in a state of repair, although it was never considered of much importance as a military station. In the 16th. century it was used as a state prison during the squabbles between the factions of Episcopacy and Presbytery, adherents to the latter persuasion the persecuted.

BOARD OF TRADE. Established 1786, a Government department for regulation and general interference, some of which no doubt justified, in pretty well every form of business in the country. W.E. Gladstone was its president during much of the railway mania period. It was the forerunner of the present Department of Trade and Industry.

BO'NESS. Originally BURWARDSTOUN then BORROWSTOWN on a point of land, a ness, which in this case projects into the Firth of Forth. By the 17th. century, Bo'ness had a large trade with Holland and the Baltic and for the next hundred years or so was one of the busiest ports on the East Coast of Scotland. But the opening of the Forth & Clyde Canal and the building of Grangemouth docks seriously reduced its importance.

BOUCH, THOMAS 1822-1880. Hamilton Ellis describes him as an engineer with rather shadowy qualifications but considerable breadth of imagination. During his career he was resident engineer for the Stockton & Darlington Railway, manager of the Edinburgh and Northern Railway, and was associated with the Edinburgh Street Tramways Company. On the mountainous line between Barnard Castle and Tebay he was credited with the design of the Beelah Viaduct, 1000 feet long and 196 feet high, the Deepdale 740 feet by 161 high, and the Tees 732 feet long by 132 high, all of these fine railway bridges, on the strength of which he was no doubt helped in securing the commission for the first Tay and the first Forth Bridges, He became a Member of the Institute of Civil Engineers in 1858, and was knighted in 1879, the year in which his Tay Bridge was later to collapse. He died at Moffat in a state of melancholia as a result of the disaster.

Further research into Sir Thomas's life and work has revealed that he was what would nowadays be described as a "chancer".

BURNTISLAND. Bartland, Bertiland, or possibly Bruntsland, prior to 1541 belonged to Dunfermline Abbey, when a swap was done for some adjacent lands with James V. He proclaimed it a Royal Burgh in 1568. Julius Agricola in 83 AD was reputed to have recognised the site as a natural port, as did Cromwell when he made his H.Q. there in 1651. The town was fortified by the French during the Auld Alliance a century earlier, and held out against Cromwell who eventually gained entry by agreeing to rebuild the harbour. The town did a reasonable trade with Holland until the English and Scottish Union of 1603, thereafter went into a decline until the diversion of the Forth ferries from Newhaven on the Edinburgh side to Pettycur (Kinghorn) on the Fife side to Granton and Burntisland in about 1844. During the latter half of the nineteenth century with a railway opening northwards in 1848, Burntisland prospered due to a liaison between the Town Council, the Harbour Authority, and the North British Railway. Coal, shipbuilding, and holiday facilities all kept going, and more so when the Forth Bridge was opened, and railway business at the ferries ceased.

CALEDONIAN RAILWAY. This Company was incorporated in 1845 to build a line from Carlisle to Edinburgh and Glasgow. Access to the latter city, which was the more important of the two, was obtained by running over the Glasgow & Garnkirk Railway opened in 1831, and the Wishaw & Coltness, opened fully in 1842. The main line was constructed very quickly. Employing the means of the times, namely hordes of men with hand picks and shovels plus horses and blasting powder, the railway was in operation between Carlisle, Beattock and Carstairs, for the Edinburgh branch, and Glasgow, a total of about 150 miles in well under three years: about half the time it took to construct about ten miles of the A74 dual carriageway over a century later using up-to-date and massive earth-moving machinery. By building and take-overs of other companies, the "Caley" eventually owned 1,105 route miles of line when it became part of the London Midland & Scottish Railway in 1923.

CROISEAU, MONSIEUR L. It is pretty certain that it was a wise decision to entrust the sinking of the foundations and the underwater work parts of the undertaking to foreign workmen. On the Continent, works of this kind had been carried out to a much greater extent and in much more difficult locations than the Firth of Forth. About the year 1880, the firm of Hersent and Convreux were engaged on the Antwerp Harbour and their engineer-in-chief, M.L. Croiseau had the responsibility of the foundations which were in many respects similar to those of the Forth Bridge. Before this he had been engaged in contracts upon the Suez Canal and on the Danube at Vienna. It was while he was a partner with Sir Thomas Tancred that he became familiar with the British methods of working—that is the methods which we had in the nineteenth century.

EDINBURGH & GLASGOW RAILWAY. Incorporated in July 1838, the line was opened between Haymarket, Edinburgh, and Queen St., Glasgow on Feb. 21st, 1842. It was the first proper main-line

railway into Edinburgh, and became connected with the North British Railway at the latter company's terminus at the North Bridge in Edinburgh in 1847. Absorbed by the N.B.R. in 1865.

As now, the railway ran via Ratho, Winchburgh, Linlithgow, Polmont, Falkirk (High), and Bishopbriggs. When the line was opened, the *Statistical Account of Scotland* mentioned the fact that there was a service for a short time between Winchburgh and Queensferry operated by a minibus, a term one would not have expected to have been in use in those days.

EDINBURGH & NORTHERN RAILWAY. The original name for the Edinburgh, Perth and Dundee Railway which was changed in the Parliamentary Session of 1849 when it amalgamated with the Edinburgh, Leith and Granton. The two companies were connected by a steam ferry across the Firth of Forth between Granton and Burntisland. From the latter place the main line ran to Ladybank, opened in 1847, where it branched right for the Tay Ferry, opened 1848, and left for Perth, access to which being from Hilton Junction 2 miles outside. Opened 1848 as well.

FEU. A Scots term of Old French derivation for the right to the use of land or property in perpetuity for a stated annual payment.
    Lately many feus have been commuted for a final lump sum.

FORTH ROAD BRIDGE. Opened on 4th September, 1964.

FRAUGHT. Freight, especially that carried on a ship.

FRITH or FIRTH. A river mouth or sea inlet, especially in Scotland. Similar to fiord.

GREAT NORTHERN RAILWAY. The Company was incorporated in 1844 being an amalgamation of the London and York and the Great Northern. The main line was from Kings Cross northwards through Hitchen, Peterborough, Grantham and Doncaster. A few miles further it joined the North Eastern Railway at Shaftholme Junction. From here the GN had running powers for some 28 miles to York.

HARRISON, THOMAS 1808-1888. Civil Engineer who worked with Stephenson and became chief engineer of the York, Newcastle and Berwick Railway.

Designed Jarrow (1858) and Hartlepool Docks. President Inst. C.E. 1874.

HUDSON, GEORGE 1800-1871. Known as the "Railway King" Hudson was probably the most famous or infamous entrepreneur the country has ever had. He inherited £30,000, a vast sum at the time, and invested it in railway speculations and in ancillary businesses, all of which became veritable gold mines. In the days before rapid transport for mail and in the absence of telephones and typewriters, he managed to control railway companies which would be equivalent in size of today's London Midland Region of British Rail, and at the same time he was everywhere at once and up to his neck in the most highly advanced political and business chicanery. Commercial law was in its infancy and Hudson took full advantage of the situation but eventually over-did it.

Accused of dishonesty and sharp practice, falsification of accounts was proved against him and he was imprisoned for debt in York where he had once been Lord Mayor. Nevertheless he still retained his seat in the Commons for Sunderland, and he died in London eventually, having been helped until his demise by an annuity bought for him by loyal friends. His own millions had vanished.

JONES, JOHN PAUL 1747-1792. John Paul was born in Kirkcudbrightshire and he added the name Jones when he joined the American Navy in 1775 after having been engaged in smuggling and the slave trade in the West Indies.

With three French ships and an American one he was a threat to Edinburgh in 1779. Further naval adventures were to come whilst serving with the French and with the Russians. He died in Paris.

LARBERT. Town in Stirlingshire just north of Falkirk. The Scottish Central Railway opened the station in 1848, and it was reached a couple of years later by the Edinburgh & Glasgow opening a line from Polmont.

LATTICE GIRDER. A girder whose upper and lower horizontal members are joined together by criss-cross diagonal open strips. It has great strength combined with lightness, and is used in situations which do not always necessitate the solid plate girder.

LONDON & NORTH WESTERN RAILWAY. Founded in 1846 by an amalgamation of the Liverpool & Manchester Railway, opened 1830; the Grand Junction, opened 1837; the London & Birmingham, opened 1838; and the Manchester & Birmingham, opened 1842. It was then the longest Railway in the Kingdom—420 miles. Known by the self-appointed soubriquet of The Premier Line, by the time of the railway grouping in 1923 it comprised some forty-five formerly independent companies with a total route mileage of over two-thousand. The main lines ran from Euston to Carlisle for the West Coast Scottish connection, to Manchester and to Liverpool, and to Chester and Holyhead for the Irish service. Before the First War, the Company ran forty trains daily between London and Birmingham, of which trains ten covered the 113 miles in exactly 2 hours.

LUCIGEN LAMP. Described at the time as being the most formidable opponent of the electric arc, it was a patent form of blow-lamp and worked by forcing creosote oil (a by-product of gas) or some other kind of heavy hydro-carbon in the form of a spray through a small nozzle. The air was piped to it under pressure from a separate container and the resultant flame could be as much as 3ft. 6ins. in length. A highly dangerous contrivance by modern safety standards.

McADAM, JOHN LOUDON 1756-1836. Like Rennie and Telford he was born in Scotland but he first went to New York in 1770. He appears to have made a small fortune there; how is not clear. In 1816 he continued in road making experiments, originally begun in his native Ayrshire, whilst engaged as surveyor to the Bristol Turnpike Trust. His theory was that "it is the native soil which really supports the weight of traffic; while it is preserved in a dry state it will carry any weight without sinking."

McAdam's roads were cheaper to make than Telford's at the time, but some of Telford's have survived. The Rennies considered road-building infra dig.

MEIKLE. Mickle or muckle all mean much or a great quantity.

MIDLAND RAILWAY. The Company was formed in 1844 by the amalgamation of the North Midland, the Midland Counties, and the Birmingham and Derby Railway. For many years it was a provincial sort of system being dependent on running powers over other companies' lines for getting into London, but in 1862 it was decided to build an extension from Bedford to St. Pancras, which was opened on October 1st., 1868. To justify this extension, the Midland introduced third-class travel on all trains in 1872, which caused a sensation at the time. They introduced Pullman Cars into England in 1874. They abolished second-class in 1875 This accommodation then became third. Other railway companies had to follow suit, so that as time passed the number 2 vanished from carriage doors, leaving 1 and 3. British Rail now call the two classes first and second and only identify the firsts on their trains.

By the opening in 1875 of their line to Carlisle the Midland worked with the Glasgow & South Western to Glasgow via Kilmarnock, and with the North British via Hawick for Edinburgh and the Forth Bridge. The distance from London to Carlisle by the Midland was 308 miles, there were many stops and the route was tortuous and hilly. But the line attracted much business even for the full run, not only because of its comfortable carriages and meals, but also for the scenery traversed—an attraction which was very much plugged in their advertising posters.

MURRAY'S TIMETABLE. A note in the *Railway Magazine* for March 1936 says that this timetable began as a quarterly publication in 1842, but the owners, Thomas Murray & Co. Ltd., of Glasgow had not got an earlier copy than one dated July 1st, 1843, which was compiled by A.K.

Murray and was printed and published by Neilson & Murray, Cross, Paisley.

The vest-pocket sizes followed the A B C -style of arrangement for trains to and from Edinburgh, Glasgow etc., and at one period were called "Diaries". Originally priced at one old penny, when the last issue appeared in 1966 the price was a shilling, five new pennies. It carried an advertisement for British United "Interjet" air service to London. A complete crib in every respect of the small Murray's Edinburgh Timetable was published before the First War by Armour & Co., of Thistle St., Edinburgh.

NORTH BRITISH RAILWAY. Incorporated on the 19th July, 1844, for a line from Edinburgh to Berwick (junction with the York, Newcastle and Berwick), with a branch to Haddington. The line, 46 miles long was opened on June 18th, 1846, and during the ensuing 70 years it acquired by amalgamations etc., over fifty independent railway companies, and undertakings such as the 32 miles long Union Canal, and the Forth and Tay ferry systems.

NORTH BRITISH "ATLANTIC" LOCOMOTIVES. A famous class of engine with the 4-4-2 wheel arrangement built between 1906 and 1921. The locos all had romantic names, the last to be withdrawn being No. 9875 "Midlothian" in November 1939— probably in error as it had been earmarked for preservation.

NORTH EASTERN RAILWAY. Incorporated in 1854 as an amalgamation of the York, Newcastle & Berwick Railway, the York & North Midland which joined that city to Leeds, Selby, Hull, Bridlington, and Scarborough, and the Leeds Northern Railway which ran from Leeds to Stockton via Harrogate, Ripon, Thirsk, and Northallerton. The Stockton & Darlington which was opened in 1825, was amalgamated with the North Eastern in 1863. The previous year saw the amalgamation of the Newcastle & Carlisle, the last section of which had been completed in 1838.

NORTH QUEENSFERRY STATION. Although not apparently envisaged at the start of traffic on the Forth Bridge, the station there was built pretty soon after the opening of the railway. The minutes of the Company for 26th February 1891 says that the station cost £4,078/0s/9d.

PETTYCUR. Small seaside town between Burntisland and Kinghorn.

POLE, WILLIAM 1814-1890. Engineer, musician and an authority on whist. M.I.C.E. 1840; F.R.S. 1851; Mus.Doc. Oxford 1867, and Vice-President of the Royal College of Organists.

Assisted John Fowler amongst others as a consulting engineer in Westminster.

RAILWAY MANIA. The years 1845 to 1850 were those of the growth of commercial and competitive railway promotion in this country, and it was the era of the business gambler who had available an enormous output of literature dealing with railway finance and speculative investment. However, even before the Stockton and Darlington Railway actually got going in 1825, there is evidence of an impending mania as people foresaw possible railway capabilities. Tomlinson, in his *History of the North Eastern Railway*, quotes from newspapers of the period, mentioning twenty new railway schemes in agitation representing a capital of about £14,000,000.

Amongst them were the London Northern Railroad Company "to connect Birmingham, Derby, Nottingham, Hull and Manchester with each other, with the parts adjacent and with the metropolis". William Beil of Edinburgh to the mayor of Newcastle-upon-Tyne wrote a letter suggesting a line through his town from Edinburgh to London, on which the "*Tyne Mercury*" commented:— "of all the irrational schemes that have yet been broached surely the most absurd."

Tomlinson continues:—"Another 'grand trunk railway' between London and Edinburgh had, however, been suggested several months before this date, for the conveyance of goods and passengers by means of locomotive and stationary engines, the proposed line being taken past Bedford to Leeds, leaving, a little on the west, the towns of Northampton, Leicester, Loughborough, Nottingham, Mansfield, Chesterfield, Sheffield and Barnsley, and, on the east, Huntington, Stamford, Worksop, Doncaster and York, and, in its course northward of Leeds, passing at nearly equal distances between Carlisle and Newcastle." The nation was said to be 'railway-mad' and "unquestionably", wrote Edward Baines in the "*Leeds Mercury*" of 24th December, 1824, "the rage of speculation has taken so decided a turn in this direction, as to present several symptoms of the popular delusion which sometime arises out of a strong and general excitement of the most active passions of human nature."

The Mania of the 1840's knew no bounds. Lord Claricarde in the House of Lords in 1845 said that Charles Guernsey, the son of a charwoman, engaged as a clerk in a broker's office at twelve shillings a week (60p), had his name down as a subscriber for shares in the London and York line for £25,000. Thackeray's C. Jeams De La Pluche, Esq., a burlesque, told his master, Sir George Flimsy, a banker in the city, that he had been speculating in railways and had won £30,000.

RASTRICK, JOHN URPETH 1780-1856. Was a partner of John Hazeldine of Bridgnorth in the building of locomotives, which included the "Catch-me-who-can" for Richard Trevithic in 1808. In civil engineering he built an iron bridge over the Wye at Chepstow in 1816, and in a letter to the Navy Office in 1816 he criticised the method of shipping stone for the building of Plymouth Breakwater. He was judge for the Liverpool & Manchester Railway at the Rainhill Trials which resulted in a prize for George and Robert Stephenson's "Rocket" in 1829.

Along with Foster he built three locomotives for America in 1828, and was resident engineer for the London & Brighton Railway until 1846. He did a great deal towards the introduction of railways in the pioneering days and his famous Note Book contains much useful first-hand information and diagrams for locomotive historians. He retired in 1847. Member of the Institution of Civil Engineers, 1827, and a Fellow of the Royal Society in 1837.

RENNIE, GEORGE 1791-1866, JOHN 1761-1821, and JOHN 1794-1874. Famous family of civil engineers who between them ran a vast business which covered shipbuilding and harbour work, early railways, canals, and drainage. They built the famous Plymouth Breakwater, old Southark and old Waterloo Bridges, and the younger John was knighted on the completion of London Bridge in 1831.

SCOTT, SIR WALTER 1771-1832. Scottish novelist and poet. A lawyer, he would rise at 5 o'clock in the morning and finish writing at noon, the rest of the time being spent at his legal business and possibly somewhat extravagant recreation and socialising. His output was phenomenal even during failing health when in 1825 he began to pay off the enormous debt of honour of £130,000, the result of the financial collapse of his partner and publisher. He was made a Baronet in 1820.

He was master of the then new historical adventure tale when the whole of the English speaking world was ready for it, and he made a fortune. "If much of what he wrote is no longer readable, at least *THE ANTIQUARY* and *OLD MORTALITY* deserve to live on." The North British Railway "J" class of *4-4-0* locomotives were named after his characters, and Waverley Station, Edinburgh, perpetuates his novel of 1814. He was reputed to have been an original shareholder in the Liverpool & Manchester Railway of 1830.

SKEWBACK. A civil engineering term. *Chamber's Technical Dictionary* says:— "The part of a pier which immediately supports a segmental arch Its upper bed is inclined towards the centre of the arch, to correspond with those of the voussoirs, while its lower bed is horizontal, to correspond with those of the stones in the pier." A voussoir is an arch-stone shaped like a wedge.

STEPHENSON, ROBERT 1803-1859. Son of George, he was apprenticed to a coal viewer, i.e. a colliery manager, at Killingworth near Newcastle-on-Tyne, when he was sixteen years of age.

Was at Edinburgh University for six months in 1822. Assisted his father on the Stockton & Darlington Railway, and later became manager of his father's locomotive works at Newcastle where he was the brains behind "Rocket", George being absent most of the time on constructing the Liverpool & Manchester Railway.

After a spell abroad in South America with the Colombian Mining Association, he found fame and fortune in his own right notably with his railway bridges, Conway, 1848; Menai, 1850; High Level at Newcastle, 1849; Royal Border, Berwick, 1850; and at Montreal in 1859.

He was M.P. for Whitby 1847-1859, President Inst. C.E. 1856-1857; Fellow of the Royal Society, 1849; Doctor of Civil Law, Oxford, 1857; and also received Norwegian and Belgian honours. He married Fanny Sanderson in 1829, and had no children. Descendants of George Stephenson therefore are from Robert's cousins.

When Queen Victoria opened the Royal Border Bridge, Robert Stephenson was offered a knighthood but he refused it.

He is buried in Westminster Abbey.

TELFORD, THOMAS 1757-1834. Civil engineer. The "Colossus of Roads". Originally apprenticed to a stone-mason, he eventually constructed over 10,000 miles of road and 1,200 bridges, his most famous works being the road from London to Holyhead which included the Menai Suspension Bridge (1825), the Dean Bridge, Edinburgh (1832), the Caledonian Canal (1803-1823), the St. Katherine's Dock in London (1826-1828).

Late in life he submitted a design for the Clifton Suspension Bridge which was hopelessly bizarre, not the sort of effort he would have produced in his younger days.

He was the first president of the Institution of Civil Engineers, a Fellow of the Royal Society, and is buried in Westminster Abbey. Telford New Town in Shropshire is named after him.

TREVITHICK, RICHARD 1771-1833. Was the undoubted inventor of the steam locomotive. Whilst employed as a technical advisor to the managers of the Cornish tin-mining industry Trevithick devised the first steam engine which could be put on wheels in order to propel itself. With James Watt's enormous engines with separate condensor and using a mixture or combination of low pressure steam and atmospheric pressure the machines could never be anything other than stationary. Trevithick's locomotives used high pressure steam, were of light weight, and could run on rails. His first one was built at Pen-y-darren in 1804, his second at Gateshead for the Wylam Colliery in 1805, and the third at Bridgnorth for exhibition in London in 1808 ("Catch me who can").

WAVERLEY, Cecil Woodham-Smith says that Scott took the name from Waverley Abbey, near Farnham, the house of Mrs Nicholson, Florence Nightingale's aunt.

INDEX